Acknowledgements

This book would not have been possible without large contributions from numerous people.

The foundation chapters on which the book is based rely heavily on the real dataset kindly made publicly available by Mala Maini. We are firm believers that practical, hands-on learning works best, and Mala's generosity in making this available to us, and the general public, is very much appreciated. Likewise, her consent to making a flow cytometry file publicly available to form part of the Recipes chapter is also appreciated.

We are also indebted to Jemima Thomas, Alice Burton and Leo Swadling for ensuring programming examples can all be successfully reproduced, for improving the quality of the content of the book, and for general proof reading.

Niclas is extremely grateful to Benny Chain for sparking his interest in the analysis of immunological data during his PhD, and for his expert tutelage throughout his time in academia along with John Shawe-Taylor. Likewise, Trevor Craven played a big role in shaping Niclas' mathematical thinking throughout his school years, for which he is appreciated.

Laura's interest in pursuing a career in immunology as a bench scientist began whilst working for GSK as part of her undergraduate degree and continues to grow in Mala's lab at UCL. Being part of the 'Mainiacs' has been so much fun and greatly contributes to a passion for research and science communication.

We are both extremely grateful to our parents, Julian and Linda Thomas and Kevin and Jane Pallett, for their continued love and support throughout our lives.

Finally, we are both very grateful for the significant amount of support given by the British Society for Immunology (BSI), providing substantial publicity and assistance with marketing to ensure immunologists are aware of this book's existence. Laura has been a member of BSI for many years, and appreciates their continuous support throughout her career.

About Us

Niclas Thomas MMath MRes PhD

Niclas is a professional data scientist with experience at several large retailers, tackling a wide range of business problems using advanced mathematical and statistical techniques.

Niclas gained his PhD at UCL using machine learning to build predictive models of the immune system, combining standard experimental techniques with advanced analytical methods. These methods were applied to a variety of data types, from high throughput sequencing data to lower dimensional cell frequency data. Following completion of his PhD, he worked as a postdoctoral research scientist at the Institute of Immunity and Transplantation, UCL, using machine learning to predict renal transplant failure from flow cytometry data.

Whilst academic data science differs to corporate data science on a couple of points, such as scope for innovation and pace of delivery, there are far more similarities than differences. Both require sound theoretical knowledge, the ability to programmatically implement mathematical ideas, a collaborative mindset and the ability to communicate complex approaches and results to non-technical colleagues. The last of these points is a particular passion of his.

Niclas continues to consult on several academic immunological projects, advising on statistical analysis, experimental design and visualisation techniques amongst other things. As well as improving the quality of data analysis, he enjoys bringing data science to new audiences, and this book and associated website is written with this in mind.

Laura Pallett BSc PhD

Laura is a postdoctoral research scientist at UCL, focussing on understanding the mechanisms of immune dysfunction in the context of chronic hepatitis B infection. Having gained a PhD in viral immunology with first-author publications in Nature Medicine and Journal of Experimental Medicine, she is now continuing to investigate immunological mechanisms at play in the human liver, with interests in immunometabolism and tissue-residency.

Having trained as a laboratory scientist, she continues to conduct her research in a lab environment. However, more recently she has taken a keen interest in advanced methods to analyse immunological datasets. In particular, she believes that strong fundamentals in statistics coupled with practical knowledge of visualisation techniques is now a must for the modern immunologist.

Laura is passionate about science communication, and is the co-founder and co-author of her lab's twitter feed, with the aim of bringing their work to a broader audience. She is also an early careers representative on the British Society of Immunology Forum.

Contents

1 Introduction   **13**
    1.1 The Data Explosion 13
    1.2 The Data Explosion in Immunology 15
    1.3 What Is Data Science? 16
    1.4 What is Data Science for Immunologists? 18
    1.5 Who Is This Book For? 19
    1.6 Who Isn't This Book For? 20

2 Organising   **23**
    2.1 Data Provenance 23
    2.2 Guiding Principles 24

3 Programming   **29**
    3.1 So Many Languages, So Little Time 29
    3.2 Bilingual is Best 30
    3.3 Basics 31
       3.3.1 Prerequisites 31
       3.3.2 Basic Operations 32
       3.3.3 Types of Variables 34
    3.4 Putting the Basics into Practice 36
    3.5 Data Frames 41
    3.6 Functions 44
    3.7 Plotting 46
       3.7.1 Bar Plot 47
       3.7.2 Grouped Bar Plot 49
       3.7.3 Boxplot 50

	3.7.4 Violinplot	51
	3.7.5 Scatterplot	52
	3.7.6 Heatmap	54
	3.7.7 Histogram	54

4 Statistics — 57
- 4.1 What is a p-value? — 57
- 4.2 Parametric vs. Non-Parametric Statistical Tests — 58
  - 4.2.1 t-test — 59
  - 4.2.2 Mann-Whitney U test — 60
- 4.3 How Can We Compare More Than Two Groups? — 61
  - 4.3.1 One-Way ANOVA — 63
  - 4.3.2 Two-Way ANOVA — 64
- 4.4 Correlation vs. Regression — 66
- 4.5 Chi-squared Test — 69
- 4.6 Power Calculations — 71

5 Clustering — 75
- 5.1 What is Clustering? — 75
- 5.2 Centroid-Driven Clusters: K-Means Clustering — 76
  - 5.2.1 Assessing the Quality of the Clusters — 79
- 5.3 Linkage-Driven Clustering: Hierarchical Clustering — 82
- 5.4 Density-driven Clustering: DBSCAN — 84
- 5.5 Distribution-driven Clustering: Gaussian Mixture Models — 86
- 5.6 How to Choose the Correct Number of Clusters? — 89
- 5.7 Which Clustering Method Should I Use? — 90

6 Dimension Reduction — 93
- 6.1 The Shrewd Photographer — 93
- 6.2 Linear Dimension Reduction: Principal Component Analysis — 95
- 6.3 Non-linear Dimension Reduction — 99
  - 6.3.1 Isomap — 99
  - 6.3.2 t-SNE — 101
- 6.4 Supervised Linear Dimension Reduction: Linear Discriminant Analysis — 103

7 Predicting — 107

- 7.1 Assessing Model Accuracy 108
  - 7.1.1 Continuous Outcome: Root Mean Square Error (RMSE) 108
  - 7.1.2 Continuous Outcome: Mean Accuracy Percentage Error (MAPE) 108
  - 7.1.3 Continuous Outcome: R^2 109
  - 7.1.4 Categorical Outcome: Accuracy, False Positive Rate and False Negative Rate 109
  - 7.1.5 Categorical Outcome: Area Under Curve (AUC) 110
  - 7.1.6 F1 Score 112
- 7.2 Frameworks to Calculate Accuracy Metrics 112
- 7.3 Predicting Continuous Outcomes 114
  - 7.3.1 Linear Regression 114
  - 7.3.2 Random Forests 117
- 7.4 Predicting Binary Outcomes 120
  - 7.4.1 Support Vector Machine 121
  - 7.4.2 Logistic Regression 127
- 7.5 Predictions with Text 130
- 7.6 Feature Selection 132

8 Recipes   137
- 8.1 Gene Expression 137
- 8.2 Flow Cytometry 143
- 8.3 Sequencing 149

Chapter 1

Introduction

1.1 The Data Explosion

It is difficult to overhear the word 'data' today without it being preceded by 'big', and with good reason. We live in an age where data is available from more and more sources and in greater volume and frequency than ever before. Retailers want to know more about the behaviour of each of their customers, insurers want to better understand the risk associated with a potential client and clinicians are constantly seeking better ways to understand their patients. Whatever the goal, acquiring data is essential. Without it, we know nothing about our customer, client or patient.

Although it may seem that data became 'big' only recently, an awareness of unmanageable amounts of data as a resource has been well understood for many years - the term 'information explosion' was first coined in the 1940s [1]. Since then, a number of colourful metaphors have been used to describe this trend, including 'data is the new oil' [2] and 'data glut' [3]. Nowadays, 'big data' appears to be the fashionable way to refer to this phenomenon, although the term itself can mean different things to different people.

For some, big data as a phrase can be taken at face value, simply meaning a large amount of data either in terms of the number of *features* or the number of *observations*. Data is often thought of as a 'table' (often called a dataframe in the context of programming, as we shall see in later chapters) containing rows and columns of values (which can be numeric or text). The rows typically represent an *observation* such as a customer or patient. Columns typically represent the *features* of a customer or patient, such as age, gender or height. Thus, big data in this case would entail either a large number of patients, a large number of details available for each patient, or both. Exactly how many patients would constitute a 'big' dataset is contentious and arbitrary. As a guide, I would consider approximately 1 million patients as large, and perhaps more than 100 features. These figures are of course subjective and dependent on the context - data on 1000 patients as part of a clinical trial may be considered big, yet data on 1000 customers for a multi-national retailer is unlikely to be considered big.

Related to this is the relationship between the number of features in a dataset and the number of observations. This is classically know as the curse of dimensionality, and is a well-studied concept in machine learning. In mathematical terminology, this is referred to as $n >> p$, meaning n is a lot bigger than p, where p represents the number of observations and n represents the number of features - in other words, many more features than observations. Nowadays, with current technology such as Cytof and gene expression profiling, the presence of more features than observations is becoming increasingly common. For example, typical gene expression profiling datasets consist of thousands of genes [4, 5], yet due to patients being notoriously difficult to recruit to studies, the number of observations rarely creeps above 100. Likewise, with the advent of next generation sequencing, an astounding number of features exists within the DNA sequences of more than 10^7 T cell receptors [6, 7], which can be routinely achieved with MiSeq. Fortunately, mathematical techniques exist that can cope with the so-called curse of dimensionality. We shall see in later chapters that support vector machines are well-equipped to make accurate, efficient predictions on thousands of features even when the data has come from only a small number of patients. Likewise, statistical approaches exist to deal with the investigation of many variables sequentially by using the correction for multiple hypothesis testing.

In bygone days, a few megabytes of data might have sufficed due to limitations in data storage and analysis. We may have recruited a relatively small group of patients to a clinical trial and hoped to obtain meaningful statistical conclusions from a cohort with limited power. Nowadays, terabytes of data has become the norm in a world where data storage is not even a minor concern, never mind a headache. The ease at which large amounts of data can now be trivially stored has in turn driven demand for the next cog in the data machine - data science.

1.2 The Data Explosion in Immunology

With the advent of several 'omics' technologies, life sciences have well and truly entered the 'big data' era; and the field of immunology is far from immune. Significant advances in technology and instrumentation throughout the 20th century, alongside enhanced sample collection, processing and immunological assays have facilitated the transition into the 'big data era'.

It is worth taking a step back momentarily to appreciate the infancy of the field of immunology. Many would argue the beginnings of 'immunology' can be traced back to Edward Jenner and the discovery of the smallpox vaccination in 1796 [8]. Since the turn of 20th century, over 30 scientists have been recognised with Nobel Prizes for outstanding contributions to understanding the immune system. In fact, the first Nobel Prize for physiology or medicine was awarded to an immunologist in 1901 to Emil Adolf von Behring, for his work detailing the use of serum therapy to treat cases of diphtheria [9].

More recently, technological advances such as the movement from base-by-base sequencing using Sanger sequencing to next generation sequencing (NGS) have enabled experimental questions relating to DNA structure like never before [10]. NGS platforms can now sequence more than 45 genomes in a day at a cost of less than $1000 per sequence. In 2005 an Illumina genome analyser could produce 1 Gbp (giga base pairs) of data in a single run. Nine years later, this rate increased to 1.8 Tbp (tera base pairs) in a single run, facilitating the discovery of genetic variants of immune-related illnesses with relative ease. Personalised medicine based on an individual's genetics is no longer a dream. Advances in sequencing technology have not benefited genome analysis alone. T and B cell repertoire analysis is hitting new heights due to the quality of sequencing data that is now produced. Recent studies have revealed fascinating insights into the adaptive immune repertoire like never before [11, 12, 13, 14]. However, this greater capability in acquiring information on immune repertoire sequences places greater requirements on careful, innovative data analysis to avoid such pitfalls as missing rare clones [15] and underestimating total diversity [16].

In addition to sequencing, flow cytometry has also progressed significantly over the past few decades. The first patent relating to flow cytometry was filed in 1949 by Wallace Coulter as a method for primarily counting red-blood cells suspended in fluid [17]. Flow cytometry then went on the exploit the principles of laminar flow to give rise to analysers still in use today. Continued development throughout the 1960s led to the finding that fluorescent chemicals (fluorochromes) conjugated to antigens of interest, could be excited into emitting lights at longer wavelengths than the initial source of light which could be detected and converted to electrical signals. These electrical signals, once decoded, provide the numerical data from which immune cell populations can be defined. The ongoing development of both hardware and chemical backbones for use in fluorochromes has increased the number of immune parameters (i.e. markers) that can be measured at a single cell level. While this increase in available parameters may cause concern amongst some immunologists over spectral overlap, the introduction of mass cytometry in 1983 has at least begun to address some of these challenges by using metal atoms as tags rather than fluorochromes and atomic mass spectrometry as the detector. This approach allows the detection of up to 100 distinguishable tags [18], providing gigabytes of 'big' data' in a single run.

1.3 What Is Data Science?

Whilst no single definition of data science exists, it broadly concerns the application of the scientific method to data. Data science is used to obtain insights from data through a combination of advanced analytical techniques from several fields, acting at the intersection of statistics, mathematics, machine learning and programming.

Machine learning in particular has seen a huge growth in interest recently, and whilst the hype may not always live up to reality, recent advances in this field allow novel insights to be drawn from data like never before. The phrase 'machine learning' was coined in 1959 by Arthur Samuel [19], defining it as a field of study that gives computers the ability to learn without explicitly being programmed. Whilst this is an apt description when taken literally, it can perhaps at first seem rather difficult to accept that such a thing may be possible. Machine learning allows us to recognise patterns in data, and consequently take action based on those patterns. For example, we may have a dataset describing thousands of clinical measurements taken from hundreds of patients - machine learning can allow us to determine which of those measurements are most important in determining a patient's prognosis. Machine learning and artifical intelligence are closely related, but subtley different, and the exact differences in definition that you hear will depend on who you ask. As far as we are concerned, artifical intelligence is the more generic term applied to the machines themselves that are capable of behaving like a human on some level. Machine learning is the set of algorirthms that give the machine 'intelligence'.

Knowledge of the two paradigms of statistics (frequentist and Bayesian) is also a key part of a data scientist's skillset. Bayesian statistics (named after Thomas Bayes) is the general paradigm centred on the degree of belief in any event, known as Bayesian probabilties, where *prior probability* and *evidence* are used to calculate the *posterior* probability. For example, if a patient presents in clinic we may have a *prior* belief of how likely they are to have tuberculosis (based on prevalence rates in the local region and perhaps further demographic factors such as previous history, age and gender). If the clinician then learns that they have recently travelled to sub-Saharan Africa, the *evidence* the clinicians have garnered will lead us to update our *posterior* probability, and we will likely conclude that it is increasingly likely that they have tuberculosis. Finally, if further evidence is provided (by means of clinical testing, such as a biological culture to confirm disease presence), then the clinician will again update their *posterior* probability and conclude that it is highly likely that the patient has tuberculosis.

Frequentist statistics, on the other hand, is most typically used to evaluate a hypothesis - so-called statistical hypothesis testing. All immunologists are familiar with the notion of a t-test, although it may be fair to say that not all immunologists are fully aware of what a p-value really is [20]. Frequentist statistics is based on the paradigm that we can work out how likely a particular event is under a certain statistical model. If we deem the event to be unlikely under such a model, then we reject our so-called null hypothesis. Although widespread in many fields of research, not least immunology, the field of frequentist statistics is not without its critics, where the debate centres around the use and misuse of p-values [20], and I would encourage any curious reader to do some further reading on what is an interesting topic.

Knowledge of theoretical techniques in machine learning, statistics and mathematics means little without the power to implement them. For this reason, the ability to programme and implement established algorithms, alongside original approaches to analyse data, is absolutely critical. Without this skill, a data scientist has to rely on off-the-shelf software that stifles creativity and limits potentially novel findings being drawn from the dataset. Data scientists may occsasionally produce code that goes straight into professional use (e.g. being used as part of a website), but usually the cycle is more complex than that, requiring professional software engineers to make the original prototype code more robust and ready for use by the general public.

The best data scientists are those with a sound knowledge of machine learning and statistical techniques, combined with strong programming skills. Data scientists with these skills have never been in such high demand, reflected both in the number of roles available and the remuneration packages on offer. Data science in particular has benefited greatly from becoming the oil [2] and soil [21] of the 21st century, and the role of a data scientist has also been perceived to be the sexiest job of this century [22]. This has to some extent been driven by numerous companies seeking an edge over rival businesses, in turn forcing smaller companies to play catch-up.

1.4 What is Data Science for Immunologists?

The demands of data science in a business setting are very different to those in an immunological research setting. For example, the practice of web scraping (automating the retrieval of information from web pages) is commonly required in a business setting, but is usually an irrelevant skill in the context of immunology. For this area of research, data science requires a heavy focus on frequentist statistics (i.e. statistical significance testing), visualisation techniques (i.e. dimension reduction, clustering and alternative methods to display information) and the use of predictive modelling.

Data Science for Immunologists places more emphasis on relevant techniques, ignoring methods that will likely never be needed and instead focussing on those that should form the backbone of an immunologist's analytical toolkit. The field of immunology itself is complex and diverse, and it can be difficult to keep up-to-date with emerging immunological concepts without additionally staying up-to-date with emerging concepts in data science. For this reason, immunologists often rely on consulting a mathematician or bioinformatician when complex data analysis is required. Indeed, this was the context in which we as authors met. Both have observed first-hand the success of applying data science techniques to immunological data with publications in *Nature Medicine*, *Journal of Experimental Medicine* and *Bioinformatics* amongst many others.

Furthermore, a lack of programming experience results in a reliance on off-the-shelf, commercial software such as GraphPad Prism or FlowJo to analyse data. This is understandable, given that no specialist skills are required to use such commercial software that have point-and-click, graphical user interfaces (GUI). Basic I.T. competency is all that is required to use these off-the-shelf tools. From conducting simple power calculations to determine sample size, to advising on the correct statistical approach to determine significance, through to building complex predictive models, an immunologist needs knowledge of mathematical techniques to produce high impact, cutting-edge research. Whilst some research labs may be able to call on the expertise of a resident bioinformatician, this is not always the case. Without these expertise to call on, an ignorance of data science techniques can be detrimental to producing and publishing high quality research; the only solution in these cases is to gain the ability to implement statistical analyses independently.

1.5 Who Is This Book For?

If you are an immunologist who has ever felt unsure of what mathematical techniques exist to analyse your data, then this book is certainly for you. Likewise, if you are aware of some data science technqiues but are unsure when and exactly how to use them, then you will also benefit from reading this book. If you have felt limited by using techniques only made available through such commercial software as FlowJo or GraphPad Prism and would like to learn how to program your own code to perform your own analysis, then this book is for you.

The techniques presented in this book will be multi-purpose and applicable for other research disciplines, but all of the examples presented will be based on real immunological data that has been made publicly available to download. All examples will be presented with the corresponding code, allowing the reader to replicate any analysis should they wish. More importantly, this corresponding code will be fully explained so that the reader can develop a solid grounding for programming their own analyses, even if they have no prior experience of programming.

Textbooks that focus on data science as a general skill set may not be particularly relevant for the everyday researcher. Practical and relevant knowledge of power calculations, fundamental statistics and core machine learning concepts is, however, an absolute necessity as we move into a world of 'big data'. This book is aimed at bridging the knowledge gap, introducing some of the most relevant data science techniques for immunologists. Specifically, this book is aimed at anyone who wants to learn fundamental mathematical techniques to complement and hopefully improve their current analyses.

By the end of the book, you should have acquired: -

- Core programming skills and the ability to begin coding basic analyses.
- Practical understanding of the most popular data science techniques in clustering, making predictions and dimension reduction.
- Knowledge of fundamental statistical tests along with an understanding of when and how to apply them.
- Advanced analytic recipes with associated code to implement techniques learnt in the early chapters.

1.6 Who Isn't This Book For?

I believe there is a clear distinction between bioinformatics and data science for immunologists. The former is concerned with a strong working knowledge of software tools specifically developed for the purpose of analysing biological and immunological data. For example, the ability to use command line tools to process and analyse $-omics$ datasets is a key part of a bioinformatician's armoury. Data science techniques, on the other hand, are transferable to many contexts, from immunology to banking, retail and beyond. As the title of the book suggests, we will only be introducing concepts from data science, although that's not to say that bioinformatic tools are not as important. For anyone specifically looking to learn about bioinformatic tools, we would suggest other resources written by authors with far more expertise in the area of bioinformatics than us - excellent books in this area include *Bioinformatics: An Introduction* by Jeremy Ramsden and *Introduction to Mathematical Methods in Bioinformatics* by Alexander Isaev.

This book is also not aimed at researchers who are already competent programmers and have basic working knowledge of at least two of the following topics; statistics, clustering, dimension reduction or making predictions. In such cases, I would recommend more advanced books such as the classic *The Elements of Statistical Learning* by Jerome H. Friedman, Robert Tibshirani and Trevor Hastie or *Algorithms for Data Science* by Brian Steele, John Chandler and Swarna Reddy. For more practical, hands-on learning, I would recommend *Python for Data Analysis* by Wes McKinney or *R for Data Science* by Garrett Grolemund and Hadley Wickham.

Chapter 2

Organising

In some ways, the way in which a researcher chooses to structure their *in silico* work is a subjective and personal choice, and one may argue that there is no right or wrong way to organise how you work. However, there are some guiding principles that must be adhered to regardless of personal preferences, and it is worth reminding the reader of these principles. Even a seasoned, experienced researcher can benefit from a review of the way in which they organise their work flow.

2.1 Data Provenance

Bench scientists will be aware of how to conduct laboratory experiments in the correct manner. This typically involves the use of positive and negative controls and full documentation of protocol to ensure the validity and reproducibility of experiments. Each experiment should at the very least detail which patient each sample comes from, for example, so that samples can be tracked back to demographic and clinical details of the patient for further analysis.

Likewise, it is important that a similar approach to science extends from the laboratory to the computer - each analysis must be carefully documented so that they can be reproduced at any time. For example, if you have developed a pipeline to perform automated gating on a flow cytometry data set (see Chapter 8 for examples), then you should document the exact approach to automated gating that was used, as you may change the gating strategy at a later date. It is of course difficult to know which gating strategy is best at first - the scientific approach requires testing multiple hypotheses and using different approaches before deciding on a suitable path to continue. Thus, scientific research will undoubtedly generate numerous outputs that ultimately go unused or unpublished. That is not to say that they should be discarded, but rather they should be archived in a sensible, consistent manner so that they can be easily referred to in the future if required. This can be achieved by following a small set of straightforward principles.

2.2 Guiding Principles

The guiding principles presented in this section are dervied from several years experience in both academic and corporate data science environments. In particular, they draw heavily on the approach of Enda Ridge's excellent Guerilla Analytics [23], a proven approach in a corporate environment where the focus is on reproducibility and readability. Whilst some of the finer details of Guerilla Analytics are not relevant for data science in an academic setting, a number of ideas transfer very well to such a setting.

One of the most important mantras is that 'time is expensive, space is cheap'. This means that trawling through old analyses trying to find that piece of analysis that you did six months ago is not an efficient use of time. Computational space is now relatively cheap. Research groups generating larger data sets may prefer to store data on a server rather than locally on a machine, with server space available at a good price. Thus, efficiency in time should be prioritised over efficiency in space - if replicating your data and analyses across several folders means you can easily find each analysis you've ever done for a project, then so be it.

Another key principle is a clear, concise folder structure on your machine. Some readers may have given plenty of thought to how best to organise the files and folders that build up as your project progresses. For others, such attention may be deemed unnecessary, preferring an *ad hoc* approach to organising and archiving your work with no obvious structure. Some aspects of organising your work are of course subjective, and what works for you may not work for everyone. However, I strongly recommend using the following structure for each project:-

- `data` - contains all of the raw data that you generate during the project,

- `playground` - contains all of the raw code and associated files used to analyse your raw data,

- `outputs` - contains all significant checkpoints in your project's history.

The `data` folder is perhaps the most self-explanatory. All raw data generated is housed here, such as flow cytometry *.fcs* files or sequencing *.fastq* files. However, it is not just raw data that belongs in this folder; formatted data pre-analysis should also be stored here. For example, you may have received a raw microarray data set in a *.csv* format whose columns you want to rename. In this instance, if renaming columns is all that is done, the formatted data after renaming columns should also sit in the `data` folder.

Each set of data that originates from a different source should be kept in a distinct, sensibly labelled subfolder within `data`. For example, the files *my_flow_cyto_data.fcs* and *my_microarray_data.csv* will originate from different sources, so they belong in different subfolders. Sensibly labelled subfolders might look something like *data_001*, *data_002* and so on. Figure 2.1 demonstrates how this approach looks in practice.

Finally, each sub folder should have what is called a README file. In this context, the README file should contain at the very least the date on which the data was generated. It is good practice to include them in each subfolder. If you want to be thorough and adopt good practices from the outset, you should also look to include further details of the experiment, such as experimental setup, controls used, or other relevant information. More generally, README files are used to explain what a particular piece of code does.

The `playground` folder is the space to put anything that contributes to your analysis. This usually will mean the code you have written. Again, this is fairly straightforward. If you are storing these folders on a shared server where someone else may view and work on your project, then it may be worth creating a subfolder with your name. Otherwise, use this space simply to try out new ideas by writing new code. There is no worry about 'breaking' code in this folder - as soon as you have a set of code that you are happy with, it gets moved to the `outputs` folder along with relevant figures or results generated using that particular piece of code.

The `outputs` folder will contain each significant milestone that occurs during your project. This could be anything from the first draft of a paper to be published or a presentation at a lab meeting or seminar. Each of these milestones deserves a different, sensibly labelled subfolder. As with each of the `data` subfolders, it is good practice to include a README file so that you can refer back to each sub folder when required and immediately understand what its purpose was - time is expensive, space is cheap.

Finally, in addition to your folder structure following the above set of principles, your approach to naming files should be consistent. In naming your files, you should either use camel case or a combination of unicase with underscores to represent spaces. Camel case uses an upper case character for each new word and ignores spaces between words (e.g. *myFilenameInCamelCase.csv*) so that the name of the file has no space. If you find that hard to read, then the alternative is to represent spaces by using underscores, and ensure all characters are lowercase. This results in a filename such as *my_filename_in_unicase.csv*. The benefits of using one of these approaches will hopefully become clear as you begin to do more data science. Briefly, these consistent approaches to naming files limit the chance of a typo preventing your code from recognising a particular filename.

Putting all these ideas together results in a folder structure like that shown in Figure 2.1.

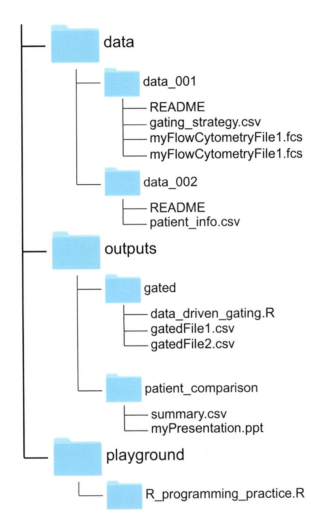

Figure 2.1: An example of a consistent, organised folder structure that is key to reproducible *in silico* work. We suggest adopting such an approach (described further in the book Guerilla Analytics by Enda Ridge [23]) to ensure data and analytic reproducibility.

Chapter 3

Programming

3.1 So Many Languages, So Little Time

A programming language is a language used to make computer programs. Computers speak a language commonly referred to as machine code. Humans, of course, speak any number of languages, but would never think of conversing in the binary language of machine code. Programming languages exist to bridge the gap between English and machine code.

Asking any programmer or data scientist for their favourite programming language is usually a recipe for disaster. In some ways it is an emotive subject, and you could find yourself subjected to a nostalgic recourse on why language X is better than language Y. That said, there are of course well-reasoned arguments for using almost any programming language, but any well-reasoned argument should be based on what you want to achieve.

As a sweeping generalisation, popular programming languages can be split into two types; production and prototyping. The general rule when comparing these two types of language is 'fast to write, slow to run' or 'slow to write, fast to run'. This means that the easier it is to translate the idea in your head to lines of code, the longer that code will take to run when you press go. Code is easier to write when it is closer to 'human' language rather than 'machine' language (i.e. hexadecimal or binary code). Conversely, the harder it is to translate your idea into lines of code, the quicker it will ultimately run on your machine. Production languages sit in the 'slow to write, fast to run' camp, while the opposite is true for prototyping languages.

Production languages such as Java and C++ are the more common choice for professional software developers when building an application that will be used by more than just its original author. The application will almost certainly have a user-interface that allows users without any prior experience or knowledge of programming to use the application. Conversely, prototyping languages such as R and Python are a more common choice for developing original ideas, taking a concept from your mind, sketching out ideas on paper and implementing those ideas on a computer. Often, these prototypes will only be used by the original developer, or the small team in which the developer is working. The prototype will almost certainly have no user-interface.

So, should you choose a production or prototyping language? Hopefully it is clear that creating professional applications with a user-interface is not the primary objective when we are conducting research. The focus of data science and analytics is on testing new ideas and translating scientific hypotheses into conclusions through machine code. A professional application with an interface is not needed to achieve this. Instead, easy to learn prototyping languages should be your weapons of choice.

3.2 Bilingual is Best

Whilst prototyping languages are easier to learn than their counterparts, a moderate investment of your time is still needed to get to grips with the basics. The two most popular prototyping languages are Python and R, and with good reason. Both are relatively easy-to-learn as they are close to what we could call 'human' language, they both have extensive documentation and help forums online to assist you when you are stuck and they both have many packages contributed by the community which saves you writing your own code in many circumstances (more on this later).

Many studies have documented the greater mental dexterity of people who can speak more than one language. I can't promise the same effect for people who can write in more than one programming language, but I can promise that such people will be well placed to carry out better analyses. This is largely due to the strengths of various packages that the two communities have developed, making some tasks easier in one language than the other.

Therefore, this book will focus on recipes to use both languages to analyse your data. This may be to achieve the same result in two different ways, simply to help you learn both languages, or simply due to a task being best carried out in just one language. For example, the *openCyto* library for flow cytometry in R is fantastic if you want to perform automated gating, whilst in Python the *scikit-learn* package is brilliant for machine learning.

Before getting into some of these more complex analyses, let's start right at the beginning with the basics.

3.3 Basics

3.3.1 Prerequisites

All examples in this book will be carried out using real code, written in both R and Python. Therefore, before you start, it will be worth installing everything you need to begin programming.

If you plan to use R, you'll need to install R along with an Integrated Development Environment (IDE) called RStudio so that you can run and edit your own code and see the results from running the code. Likewise, if you plan to use Python, you'll need to install Python along with an IDE called Jupyter. Fortunately, in the case of Python, it is possible to download a single file which bundles together Python with Jupyter, which runs through any web browser.

Please see www.datascienceforimmunologists.com for more detailed instructions for installing both R and Python if required. You will need to download the file *datascienceforimmunologists.csv* from our website to run all examples yourself. Once downloaded, make a folder called *datascience* on your Desktop, and place the downloaded file in there, remembering the structure learnt in the last chapter.

Setting Up R

1. Install R, which you can download from
   https://cran.r-project.org.

2. Install RStudio, which you can download from
   https://www.rstudio.com/products/rstudio/download/.

Once these are installed, you can simply open RStudio and away you go. Code can be typed in the top left quadrant of RStudio and can be run by clicking *Run*.

Setting Up Python

1. Install Anaconda for Python 3.x (currently 3.6 at time of print), which you can download from
   https://www.anaconda.com/download/

Once you have installed Anaconda (Python bundled together with Jupyter), you can open Jupyter through your web browser by opening the Terminal (on Mac) or command prompt (on Windows) and typing the commands below into the Terminal/command prompt. On Mac, the Terminal can be found in *Applications/Utilities*, while on Windows you can find the command prompt by searching *cmd*. *path/to/your/folder* is the location you have saved the downloaded file on which all examples are based (likely to be */Users/yourname/Desktop/datascience* on a Mac or *C:/Users/yourname/Desktop/datascience* on Windows.).

1. `cd path/to/your/folder/`

2. `jupyter notebook`

Please see www.datascienceforimmunologists.com for more detailed instructions on how to start Jupyter.

3.3.2 Basic Operations

Open RStudio if you want to learn R, or Jupyter if you want to learn Python, so that we can get started. Perhaps the simplest place to start when learning a new programming language is simple arithmetic.

Throughout this book, all Python code will be shown in yellow while R code will be shown in blue.

```
1  x = 1 + 2
```

```
1  x = 1 + 2
```

This action simply sums those two numbers together, and assigns the result to the variable *x*. There are two important lessons here. Firstly, we can add two numbers together in a very intuitive way, by using the + character. Secondly, assigning values to a variable is a fundamental part of programming. In this case, we have chosen to call that variable *x*, but we could just as easily have called it *variable*.

```
1  variable = 1 + 2
```

```
1  variable = 1+2
```

If we want to know what the value of 1 plus 2 is, we can simply print the variable

```
1  print(variable)
```

```
1  print(variable)
```

We could have taken a different approach to calculating the sum of 1 and 2.

```
1  x = 1
2  y = 2
3  z = x + y
4  print(z)
```

```
1  x = 1
```

```
2  y = 2
3  z = x+y
4  print(z)
```

We have achieved the same result, but we have done so by assigning values to *x* and *y* first, and then calculated the sum of these two values by assigning the sum to a third variable called *z*. This highlights how we can not only assign values directly to a variable, but also assign the sum of two variables to another variable.

3.3.3 Types of Variables

In the previous section we saw how we can assign an *integer* to a variable. However, we are of course not limited to only working with integers. There are three types of variables that will form the building blocks of any analysis - *integers*, *floats* and *strings*. We have seen *integers* in action in the previous subsection - these are simply the natural numbers 0, 1, 2, 3 and so on, as well as their negative counterparts -1, -2, -3, ... *Floats* are decimal numbers such as 3.4 or 18.6. *Strings* are alpha-numeric combinations on which the usual mathematical operations such as addition and subtraction will not work, examples being *patient1* or *hepatitisB*. Note that they can be both upper and lower case, and can contain numbers as well as letters. Though they may not seem as useful on first glance as integers and floats that we can add and subtract, *strings* still have many uses - for example, we may wish to label a patient by disease state or outcome, for example. We could use the integers 0 and 1 to do this, but *strings* offer an easier link to human language as opposed to binary, machine language.

We can assign a *float* or a *string* to a variable in the same way as we previously used for integers.

```
1  x = 2.4
2  y = 'healthy'
```

```
1  x = 2.4
2  y = 'healthy'
```

Here, when programming in both R and Python, the type of the variable does not need to be explicitly stated when it is assigned; your machine is clever, and will figure it out when you run the code. This brings us to another difference between production and prototype languages - production languages generally require the type of each variable to be explicitly declared when first assigned. Generally, prototyping languages (such as Python and R), don't require the type to be explicitly declared, though it is indeed possible to do this as in the example below. Note how in both languages we can use the # symbol to denote a 'comment' - comments in programming languages are instructions that will not be carried out by the computer; they simply serve as a reminder of what a particular piece of code does. It is a good idea to get into the habit of commenting on your code wherever possible.

```
x = float(2.4) # declares x to be of type float
y = str('healthy') # declares y to be of type string
```

```
x = as.double(2.4) # declares x to be of type float
y = as.character('healthy') # declares y to be of type string
```

As a rule, I would recommend that you don't explicitly declare the type of each variable - the beauty of prototyping languages is that they are easy to use, and follow the maxim of 'fast to type, slow to run'. The benefit of languages that require explicit declaration of the type of each variable is that it is generally quicker if the machine doesn't have to spend the time figuring out what type each variable is when it first encounters a new variable.

We can perform many of the same operations on floats as we can on integers,

```
x = 2.4
print(2*x) # multiplies x by 2
y = 6.7
print(x-y) # subtracts y from x
```

```
x = 2.4
print(2*x) # multiplies x by 2
```

```
3   y = 6.7
4   print(x-y) # subtracts y from x
```

Strings are a little different, by their very nature. Several operations are useful when working with strings,

```
1   var1 = 'healthy'
2   var2 = 'un'
3   print(var2 + var1) # appends the string var1 on to the end of var2
4   print(len(var1)) # returns the number of items in var1 i.e. the number of
        characters
```

```
1   var1 = 'healthy'
2   var2 = 'un'
3   print(paste(var2,var1,sep="")) # appends the string var1 on to the end of var2
4   print(nchar(var1)) # returns the number of items in var1 i.e. the number of
        characters
```

The last line above is one of many built-in functions that R and Python provide by default. In this case, the functions `len` in Python and `length` in R return the length of the string. Depending on the context in which it is used, it will also return the length of a dictionary, list or data frame. These can all be thought of as *objects* in which you can store any number of variables, and their use is crucial in putting together your own analyses.

3.4 Putting the Basics into Practice

Imagine a scenario where we have a set of three patients and their corresponding ages. In this instance, we could assign the age of each individual to a different variable, and give the variable a suitable name that allows us to (anonymously) identify each patient.

```
1   firstPatient = 24
2   secondPatient = 56
3   thirdPatient = 65
```

```
firstPatient = 24
secondPatient = 56
thirdPatient = 65
```

However, this approach is not partiuclarly scalable, and doesn't give us a natural way of storing the collection of 3 patients as a whole. As an analogy, if we want a sensible way of storing cutlery in our kitchen, we are unlikely to keep one fork in one drawer, another fork in a separate drawer and a third fork in a cupboard. Rather, we would keep all three forks together in a cutlery drawer so that we know where to find them. That way, if we decide that we want to use all of our forks, all we have to do is search the cutlery drawer rather than the whole kitchen. This notion leads to the concept of lists.

```
myPatientAgesList = [24,56,65]
print(myPatientAgesList)
```

```
myPatientAgesList = c(24, 56, 65)
print(myPatientAgesList)
```

Rather than storing each of the patients' ages in a separate variable, we can now store all patient ages in the same variable; a list called myPatientAgesList. We can still print individual patient ages using

```
print(myPatientAgesList[0]) # prints 24, the age of firstPatient
print(myPatientAgesList[1]) # prints 56, the age of secondPatient
```

```
print(myPatientAgesList[1]) # prints 24, the age of firstPatient
print(myPatientAgesList[2]) # prints 56, the age of secondPatient
```

There are several things to note here. First of all, you'll notice that the first item in the list (i.e. the age of firstPatient) is obtained by using [integer] (e.g. [1]) after the name we gave to our list. Using brackets in this way allows us to access individual elements of the list. Secondly, you should have observed that the first item in the list (24) is actually referred to as the 0th element in the list in Python.

Python starts counting from 0, and so the first item in the list is obtained by using [0], second item in the list by [1], and so on. R counts in the rather more intuitive way, beginning at 1.

Lists serve as a very useful object in many scenarios. However, in the above example, you'll notice that there is no obvious way to know which patient is 24 years old and which patient is 56 years old. Lists do not easily offer us the scope to store patient names alongside the patient ages. This drawback leads us to the concept of dictionaries.

Dictionaries serve a similar purpose to lists, in that they allow us to store multiple variables in the same object. In addition to this, they offer a natural way to address the aforementioned limitation of lists - dictionaries allow us to store each indiviudal's name alongside their age.

```
myPatientAgesDict = {'firstPatient':24, 'secondPatient':56, 'thirdPatient':65}
```

```
myPatientAgesDict = list(firstPatient=24, secondPatient=56, thirdPatient=65)
```

Firstly, note that we define a dictionary using curly brackets {} rather than the square brackets [] that we use for lists in Python. In R, we use the list() command combined with assigning a value to each element of the list. Secondly, you'll notice now that each patient name is grouped together with their age as a pair. In a similar way to lists, we can obtain each patient's age. However, using dictionaries, we can now obtain firstPatient's age directly by using firstPatient's name. Dictionaries should be thought of as *key, value* pairs - the keys of the dictionary are the patient names (firstPatient, secondPatient, thirdPatient) and the values of the dictionary are their corresponding ages (24, 56, 65).

```
myPatientAgesDict['firstPatient'] # returns the age of firstPatient
```

```
myPatientAgesDict$firstPatient # returns the age of firstPatient
```

What is the advantage of doing this? In reality, we won't refer to patients as first-

Patient, secondPatient, thirdPatient and so on, but rather with an anonymous identifier. This anonymous identifier will likely make it hard for you to remember which element in a list refers to which patient - with lists, the order of elements is important, so you would have to remember to which patient each entry in the list refers. With dictionaries, the order is irrelevant, as it is the key that is used to get the corresponding value.

To illustrate the power that dictionaries offer, we need to intoduce two new fundamental concepts - loops and *if* statements. The most common type of loop, a *for* loop, is demonstrated in the example below.

```
for n in range(10):
    print(n)
```

```
for (n in 1:10){
    print(n)
}
```

Hopefully you can work out what the second line does here - it simply prints the value of n. But what is n in this case? A loop, in programming terminology, churns through a defined 'thing', and performs an operation on each of those 'things' in turn. In the above example, the thing is the set of numbers 0 to 9 (in Python, or 1 to 10 in R). The loop churns through these numbers, and for each of those values (here the values are called n at each iteration) prints the value of n. Hence, the operation that is performed is simply printing the number. This example may seem trivial but this is one of the most fundamental concepts in beginning your programming journey, so make sure it is clear before moving on.

A second crucial concept is the if statement. Consider the example below which builds on the previous example.

```
for n in range(10):
    if n > 5:
        print(n)
```

```
for (n in 1:10){
```

```
2    if (n > 5){
3        print(n)
4    }
5  }
```

The last line remains the same, and so does the first. We have inserted a second line that tells the machine to carry out the third line only if the second line is satisfied. In the previous example, each number from 0 to 9 (1 to 10 in R) was printed in turn. In this example, the number n will only be printed if n is greater than 5. Let's put that into practice with our previous example concerning our dictionary of patient ages.

```
1  for value in myPatientAgesDict.values():
2      print(value)
```

```
1  for (value in myPatientAgesDict){
2      print(value)
3  }
```

Here, we are still using a *for* loop, but in this case we now loop through the values in myPatientAgesDict rather than the first ten integers. We can do even better than this, and get the keys *and* the values.

```
1  for key, value in myPatientAgesDict.items():
2      print(key, value)
```

```
1  for (i in 1:length(myPatientAgesDict)){
2      print(myPatientAgesDict[i])
3  }
```

Using .items() in Python, we have been able to loop over each (key, value) pair in turn, and print both the patient's name and the patient's age. Now, suppose we only want to find those patients that are above 50 years of age, then we can use the *if* statement.

```python
for patientName, patientAge in myPatientAgesDict.items():
    if patientAge > 50:
        print(patientName, patientAge)
```

```r
for (i in 1:length(myPatientAgesDict)){
  if (myPatientAgesDict[i] > 50){
    print(myPatientAgesDict[i])
  }
}
```

Dictionaries and lists are useful structures to store small sets of basic data in, but to manage larger datasets where we have more data than just the age of each patient, we need a different type of object. This leads us to data frames.

3.5 Data Frames

Data frames offer a natural, intuitive way to think about data. Most researchers, even without any programming experience, will be familar with the notion of a spreadsheet, where we store data as a set of rows and columns. This is just what a data frame is in the context of programming; a set of rows and columns that store our data is a structured way. It is important that you begin to think about data in this way - each row represents a different observation (e.g. a different patient on each row), and each column represents various bits of information (called features) on the corresponding patient such as age, gender and weight. This is commonly referred to as 'tidy data' [24] and forms the backbone of data storage for a data scientist. Almost all algorithms in Python and R will by default assume data is stored in this way when performing calculations.

Both R and Python provide extensive functionality to work with data frames, but this is perhaps the first point where R and Python diverge in their approaches. R provides this functionality in its core package, meaning that it comes as default with R without the need to install any additional packages. Python, conversely, provides this functionality as part of an additional package called pandas.

A package, in the context of programming, is really a form of crowd-sourcing. Other programmers develop these packages so that the whole programming community can benefit from their work, without each programmer having to write everything from first principles. This means that, for example, you can read a spreadsheet in Python simply using the command read_csv without having to write hundreds of lines of code that would be otherwise necessary for you to accomplish this. We'll come back to the concept of packages in future chapters, where we will lean on code developed by the community to carry out certain analyses. For now, think of any package as code that someone else has written and allowed you to use for free, and contrast this with a proprietary model of software development (where you would be required to pay for any software that has been developed by another programmer).

Let's try reading a simple .csv file in R first, without requiring any further packages to do this. We'll work with a dataset we have made publicly available on our website at www.datascienceforimmunologists.com, detailing some 'real-life' data relating to a cohort of patients followed phenotypically, immunologically and clinically. These particular patients were sampled at routine outpatient clinics in London in Hepatitis clinics, and as such all have chronic hepatitis B infection (HBV). Variables contained in the dataset include patient ages, alanine transaminase (ALT, a marker of liver inflammation), granulocytic myeloid-derived suppressor cell (gMDSC) frequencies and eAg status amongst many others. Interested readers can learn more about the dataset and the role of arginase-1-expressing gMDSC in the regulation of immunopathology in patients with chronic HBV infection in our paper published in *Nature Medicine* [25].

```
1  myData = read.csv('/Users/yourname/Desktop/datascience/data_science_for_
       immunologists.csv', header=T, na.strings=c("","NA"))
2  head(myData)
3  dim(myData)
```

This hopefully seems quite straightforward. The first line simply reads the csv that you specify in the round brackets (*/Users/yourname/Desktop/datascience.csv*). Note that this may change depending on what operating system you are using (i.e. Mac or Windows). The second line is an R function that allows us to quickly view the top 6 lines (i.e. the head) of the csv file. The third line gives us the dimensions of the data frame (the number of rows and columns).

Now let's try the equivalent in Python.

```
import pandas

myData = pandas.read_csv('/Users/yourname/Desktop/datascience/data_science_for_immunologists.csv')
print(myData.head())
print(myData.shape)
```

Note how we need one more line of code to do this. The first line is used to tell Python that we plan to use some functionality in the `pandas` package. This is the way in which we tell Python we want to use any package, so we would equally use `import sklearn` to import machine learning functions in the `scikit-learn` package (a package that we will use later in the book). The second line uses the `read_csv` function in `pandas` to read the .csv file called *data_science_for_immunologists.csv* and store this data in Python in a data frame called *myData*. The third and fourth lines perform the equivalent operations to those in the R code above, using slightly different syntax. In the case of Python, we use `.head()` and `.shape` to access the head of a file and the dimensions of a file respectively.

Now we've loaded the data into R and Python, we can perform a few basic interrogations of the data that will serve us well in later chapters. If we want to get a list of the attributes we have data for on each patient, we can use the following line of code.

```
print(myData.columns.tolist())
```

```
colnames(myData)
```

If we want to access just one column of the data frame, we use

```
myData[['patientID']]
```

```
myData$patientID
```

Finally, both Python and R provide many functions that we can use to summarise the dataset. For example, we can calculate the mean ALT (a marker of liver inflammation) level across all patients by using

```
myData[['alt']].mean()
```

```
mean(myData$alt)
```

We'll use more of these types of functions when we delve further into analysing this dataset in the next chapter.

3.6 Functions

However, we are not just limited to using built-in functions in R and Python - we have the power to write our own bespoke functions to do whatever we please. The key purpose of functions is to save you having to repeat the same piece of code multiple times in an analysis. Instead, you can define the function once at the beginning of your analysis, and then use it as many times as you like without having to retype the code (or copy and paste it). As well as making your code more tidy and concise, it also limits the appearance of bugs and typos.

Let's begin with a simple, arbitrary function that will print "Hello!" whenever it is used (in programming terminology, when a function is used we say it has been *called*). First of all, we need to define the function

```
def say_hello():
    return "Hello!"
```

```
say_hello = function(){
  return("Hello!")
}
```

Now that we have defined our function `say_hello`, we can call our function by simply using the name we gave to it followed by ().

```
say_hello()
```

```
say_hello()
```

In our first example, the function we have created will always perform the same task (i.e. print "Hello!") whenever it is called. This is because the function takes no inputs (referred to as *arguments* in programming terminology). A more complex function can be created as follows,

```
def increase_by_one(x):
    return x+1
```

```
increase_by_one = function(x){
  return(x+1)
}
```

where our function named `increase_by_one` will add one to whatever number is provided as an argument to the function. We can then use it in a similar way to before, but this time we must provide the argument between the brackets, as below.

```
increase_by_one(2)
```

```
increase_by_one(2)
```

In this case, the argument is the integer (2), so our function will return the integer 3. Finally, we are not limited to providing just one argument to our function, we can provide as many arguments as we like and manipulate these inputs accordingly.

```
def multiply_two_numbers(x,y):
    return x*y
```

```
multiply_two_numbers = function(x,y){
    return(x*y)
}
```

Here, we are simply taking two arguments and returning their product. When we call the function below, we should get a value of 12 returned to us.

```
multiply_two_numbers(3,4)
```

```
multiply_two_numbers(3,4)
```

3.7 Plotting

Visualisations produced by your analyses are arguably the most potent way to convey your message and showcase your findings. Thus, presenting your results as clearly as possible using the correct method to show your findings, is a crucial aspect of any scientific paper or presentation.

Some aspects of visualising your results are subjective and best left to judgement in deciding how to put together your visualisation. However, there are a number of axioms to bear in mind when finalising your visuals: -

- Use colour wisely: If colour is not essential, then stick to black and white. Avoid red-green colour schemes where possible to assist the colour blind. Use a consistent colour scheme wherever possible (e.g. if you're showing different plots throughout a paper or presentation, always use the same colour to represent high values and a separate, consistent colour for low values.

- Avoid using pie charts: The human eye tends to find it more difficult to interpret pie charts as values are represented by area and not by length (as in a bar plot). Therefore, a bar plot is more appropriate in almost all circumstances, unless you are trying to represent how a cake has been divided amongst a group of people.

- Keep it simple: Unneccessary complexity in your plots will usually cloud the message, keep things simple to ensure the message is clear.

Before we start plotting, we'll need to import the relevant libraries to allow us to create professional visualisations - we'll need to do this at the start of every new session to successfully create our visualisations.

```
1  import seaborn as sns
2  import matplotlib.pyplot as plt
3  from sklearn.preprocessing import scale
4
5  %matplotlib inline
```

```
1  install.packages("ggplot2")
2  install.packages("reshape")
3
4  library(ggplot2)
5  library(reshape)
```

In R, we will only need to run `install.packages("ggplot2")` once, to install the package. Once it is installed, everytime we want to use it, we just need to put `library(ggplot2)` at the top of our code. It is also worth knowing how to save your figures. In all of the examples below, you can save the last figure you plotted by using the following commands.

```
1  plt.savefig('name\_of\_my\_plot.png')
```

```
1  ggsave('name\_of\_my\_plot.png')
```

3.7.1 Bar Plot

The classic bar plot is perhaps the most widely used visualisation in immunology, and should be used when you have one categorical variable (usually displayed on the x-axis) and one continuous variable (usually displayed on the y-axis).

```
1  fig, ax = plt.subplots()
```

```
ax = sns.barplot(x='diseaseClass', y='alt', data=myData, ci=68, palette='Set1')
ax.set_xlabel('Disease Class')
ax.set_ylabel('ALT (IU/L)')
sns.despine()
plt.show()
```

```
plotData = na.omit(myData[,c("diseaseClass","alt")])
ggplot(plotData, aes(x=diseaseClass, y=alt, fill=diseaseClass)) +
  geom_bar(position = "dodge", stat = "summary", fun.y = "mean") +
  stat_summary(fun.data = mean_se, geom = "errorbar", width=0) +
  scale_fill_brewer(palette = "Set1") +
  xlab('Disease Class') +
  ylab('ALT (IU/L)') +
  theme_classic()
```

Let's take a closer look at what each line of code does in Python to begin with. Line 1 creates figure and axis objects, which are fundamental to how plotting works in Python. Think of the figure object as your easel, and the axis object as your canvas to paint on. To create these objects in Python, we simply use the function `plt.subplots()`, and can even use this to create a figure with multiple axis objects so that we can place a different plot on each axis object. Line 2 places the `sns.barplot()` on the axis object, defining what variables to put on the x and y axes. We can supply additional arguments to the bar plot function at this stage, such as defining error bars to represent one standard deviation of the mean. This is equivalent to a confidence interval of 68% (i.e. `ci=68`). We can also define which colour palette we want to use here with `palette='Set1'`. Lines 3 and 4 are used to label the x- and y-axis respectively, and line 5 is a convenient function that can be used to strip the spines from the top and right sides of the plot, which are otherwise plotted by default. Try removing this line to see the effect it has on how the plot looks, before deciding whether you think your plots look better with or without this line. Finally, line 6 simply shows the plot on screen.

Let's now look over the R code. Line 1 is used to drop any rows of data where there are missing values. Line 2 defines what variables we want to put on the x- and y-axis, where `fill='diseaseClass'` tells ggplot which variable to use to colour the bars. Lines 3 and 4 are used to generate the bar plot and additionally include error bars (representing one standard deviation of the mean). Line 5 defines which colour palette we want to use (conveniently the Set1 palette is available in both R and Python, and makes a nice choice for plots in my opinion). Lines 6 and 7 are used to label the x- and y-axis with whatever text we choose, and finally line 8 is an optional line of code that determines in what style the plot is created (controlling such things as gridlines and spines). Try experimenting with removing this line to decide what style of plot you like best.

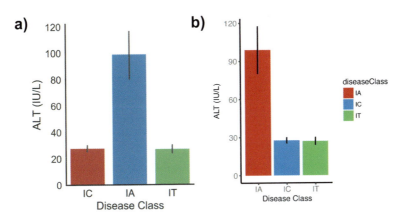

Figure 3.1: Examples of **a)** Python and **b)** R bar plots representing serum alanine transaminase levels (ALT; IU/L) by disease category (inactive carriers (IC), immune actives (IA) and immunotolerants (IT)). Error bars depict mean plus/minus one standard deviation.

3.7.2 Grouped Bar Plot

The grouped bar plot can be used to include a third, categorical variable such as gender.

```
1  fig, ax = plt.subplots()
2  ax = sns.barplot(x='diseaseClass', y='alt', hue='gender', data=myData, ci=68,
       palette='Set1')
3  ax.set_xlabel('Disease Class')
4  ax.set_ylabel('ALT (IU/L)')
5  sns.despine()
6  plt.show()
```

```
plotData = na.omit(myData[,c("diseaseClass","alt","gender")])
ggplot(plotData, aes(x=diseaseClass, y=alt, fill=factor(gender))) +
  geom_bar(position = "dodge", stat = "summary", fun.y = "mean") +
  stat_summary(fun.data = mean_se, geom="errorbar", position=position_dodge(1),
    width=.2) +
  scale_fill_brewer(palette = "Set1") +
  xlab('Disease Class') +
  ylab('ALT (IU/L)') +
  theme_classic()
```

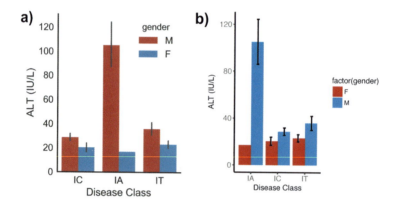

Figure 3.2: Examples of **a)** Python and **b)** R grouped bar plots representing serum alanine transaminase levels (ALT; IU/L) by disease category (inactive carriers (IC), immune actives (IA) and immunotolerants (IT)) and gender. Error bars depict mean plus/minus one standard deviation.

3.7.3 Boxplot

Whilst bar plots are commonly used when visualising categorical vs continuous variables, I would recommend using boxplots (sometimes known as box-and-whisker plots) as your default visualisation in such a scenario - boxplots include more information in the graphic as they display interquartile ranges instead of the typical error bars used for bar plots. By including the interquartile range, we get a basic understanding of the distribution of each categorical variable as well as just basic information about the mean.

```
fig, ax = plt.subplots()
```

```
2  ax = sns.boxplot(x='diseaseClass', y='alt', data=myData, palette='Set1')
3  ax.set_xlabel('Disease Class')
4  ax.set_ylabel('ALT (IU/L)')
5  sns.despine()
6  plt.show()
```

```
1  plotData = na.omit(myData[,c("diseaseClass","alt")])
2  ggplot(plotData, aes(x=diseaseClass, y=alt)) +
3  geom_boxplot(aes(fill=diseaseClass)) +
4  xlab('Disease Class') +
5  ylab('ALT (IU/L)') +
6  theme_classic()
```

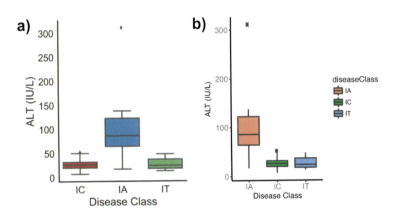

Figure 3.3: Examples of **a)** Python and **b)** R box plots representing serum alanine transaminase levels (ALT; IU/L) by disease category (inactive carriers (IC), immune actives (IA) and immunotolerants (IT)). Boxes depict upper and lower quartiles along with the median. Outliers are identified and drawn as single points using a function that depends on the interquartile range.

3.7.4 Violinplot

Violinplots take boxplots one step further by displaying the distribution of each variable explicitly in the plot itself, rather than just summary statistics of the distribution as in the case of boxplots.

```
fig, ax = plt.subplots()
ax = sns.violinplot(x='diseaseClass', y='alt', data=myData, palette='Set1')
ax.set_xlabel('Disease Class')
ax.set_ylabel('ALT (IU/L)')
sns.despine()
plt.show()
```

```
plotData = na.omit(myData[,c("diseaseClass","alt")])
ggplot(myData, aes(x=diseaseClass, y=alt)) +
  geom_violin(aes(fill=diseaseClass)) +
  xlab('Disease Class') +
  ylab('ALT (IU/L)') +
  theme_classic()
```

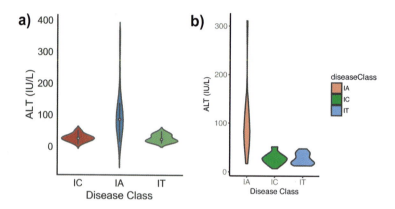

Figure 3.4: Examples of **a)** Python and **b)** R violinplots representing serum alanine transaminase levels (ALT; IU/L) by disease category (inactive carriers (IC), immune actives (IA) and immunotolerants (IT)). Violinplots show more information than a boxplot, by showing the full distribution of all points within each disease category.

3.7.5 Scatterplot

Two continuous variables are best displayed using a scatterplot, where a third variable can be used to colour each point. In this example, we use a categorical variable to colour each point, but we could also use a continuous variable to colour the points - experiment with the code below to get comfortable using the plotting library in your chosen language.

It is important to note that just because we have the capability of including additional information in the visualisation, it doesn't necessarily mean that we should. Always consider your audience and your message when deciding how to structure any graphic.

```
1  ax = sns.lmplot(x='gMDSC', y='alt', data=myData, hue='gender', fit_reg=False, size
       =4, aspect=0.9, palette='Set1')
2  ax.set_xlabels('gMDSC (%)')
3  ax.set_ylabels('ALT (IU/L)')
4  sns.despine()
5  plt.show()
```

```
1  plotData = na.omit(myData[,c("gMDSC","alt","gender")])
2  ggplot(plotData, aes(x=gMDSC, y=alt, colour=gender)) +
3    geom_point() +
4    geom_smooth(method=lm, aes(fill=gender)) +
5    scale_color_brewer(palette = "Set1") +
6    xlab('gMDSC') +
7    ylab('ALT (IU/L)') +
8    theme_classic()
```

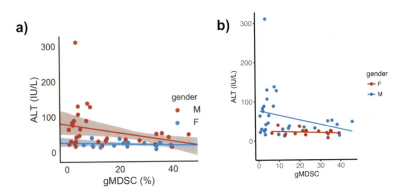

Figure 3.5: Examples of **a)** Python and **b)** R scatterplots displaying the relationship between serum alanine transaminase levels (ALT; IU/L) and frequency of granulocytic myeloid-dervied suppressor cells (gMDSC). Colour on these plots is used to display gender. Lines of best fit are shown per gender, along with shaded areas representing confidence intervals.

3.7.6 Heatmap

Heatmaps are useful graphical tools that rely entirely on colour as the means of conveying your message. As such, they cannot relay precise information to the viewer, and should generally be used only to demonstrate particular trends in your data. The intensity of the colour in each square represents the value, where more intense colours represent larger absolute values.

```python
normalisedData = scale(myData[['niScore','gMDSC']].dropna().sort_values('niScore')
    )
fig, ax = plt.subplots(figsize=(width, height))
ax = sns.heatmap( normalisedData, linewidths=0.01, cmap="bwr", xticklabels=['NI
    Score', 'gMDSC'])
ax.set(yticklabels=[])
plt.tight_layout()
plt.show()
```

```r
scaledData = na.omit(myData[,c("patientID","niScore","gMDSC")])
scaledData$niScore = scale(scaledData$niScore)
scaledData$gMDSC = scale(scaledData$gMDSC)
plotData = melt(scaledData, id="patientID")
ggplot(plotData, aes(x=variable, y=patientID)) +
  geom_tile(aes(fill=value)) +
  scale_fill_gradient2(low='blue', mid='white', high='red') +
  xlab('') +
  ylab('') +
  theme(panel.background = element_rect(fill = "white"),
    axis.ticks = element_blank(),
    axis.text.y = element_blank())
```

3.7.7 Histogram

The distribution of a single continuous variable can easily be viewed using a histogram. Note that the visual depends on how you choose your bins (the range of values on the x-axis that each rectangle represents) - larger bins will have the effect of smoothing your distribution, so use this parameter wisely when creating your graphic.

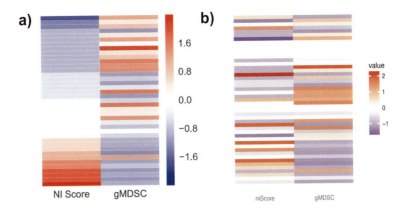

Figure 3.6: Examples of **a)** Python and **b)** R heatmaps displaying the relationship between a patient's necroinflammatory score (NI score) and frequency of granulocytic myeloid-dervied suppressor cells (gMDSC). Heatmaps show qualitative rather than quantitative trends, as a colour scale does not convey exact values. In **a)**, data has been sorted based on NI score, which can highlight a clearer trend than the unsorted NI score depicted in **b)**.

```
fig, ax = plt.subplots()
ax = sns.distplot(myData.alt, kde=False)
ax.set_xlabel('ALT (IU/L)')
sns.despine()
plt.show()
```

```
plotData = na.omit(myData$alt)
ggplot(myData, aes(x=alt)) +
  geom_histogram(binwidth=20, fill='lightblue') +
  theme_classic()
```

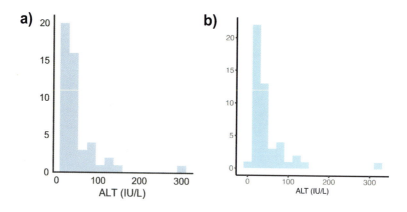

Figure 3.7: Examples of **a)** Python and **b)** R histograms representing the distribution of serum alanine transaminase levels (ALT; IU/L) across all patients.

Chapter 4

Statistics

4.1 What is a p-value?

Perhaps the most fundamental concept in analysing data, the p-value may also be the most misunderstood. In a a typical scientific experiment, we have a certain hypothesis that we wish to test, and we collect data that can help us determine whether that hypothesis is likely to be true or not. A p-value helps you to determine whether your results are significant.

To statistically test the validity of our hypothesis, we must first set the *null hypothesis*. The null hypothesis is typically a statement that no differences exist amongst the populations you wish to test. For example, suppose we have collected data describing the % of gMDSC (a particular cell type) in male and female patients with chronic hepatitis B infection, then our null hypothesis here would be that there are no differences in % of gMDSC between males and females. The *alternative hypothesis* is then simply that there are differences between the two groups.

The most common misconception with the use of p-values is that they can be used to prove the alternative hypothesis; this is not true. The way in which a statistical test is set up allows you to either accept or reject the null hypothesis, based on the evidence in the dataset that you have collected. Thus, a p-value is defined as

the probability of observing a test statistic at least as extreme as that which is actually observed, if the null hypothesis is true.

Let's take a look at that statement in a bit more detail. The test statistic will be different depending on which statistical significance test is being used. The well-known and widely used t-test uses a test statistic that compares the population means. In the example above, the test statistic when using a t-test would be the difference in mean values of the two groups (males and females). Once this test statistic has been obtained, it is used to determine whether to accept or reject the null hypothesis. If the difference in means is extreme enough, then the null hypothesis is rejected. The p-value quantifies exactly how extreme the test statistic is.

A large p-value close to one means it is very likely (i.e. a high p-value means a high probability) that we would observe the data if the null hypothesis was true. In this case, we would fail to reject the null hypothesis and conclude that there are no significant differences between the two groups. Conversely, a p-value close to zero means that it is very unlikely to have observed our actual data if the null hypothesis is true. If it is deemed sufficiently unlikely to have observed our data if the null hypothesis was true, we reject the null hypothesis and conclude there are differences in % of gMDSC between males and females.

By convention, a p-value of 0.05 is used to decide whether the differences between the two groups is sufficiently unlikely. In other words, if there is less than a 5% chance of observing our actual data if the null hypothesis is true, then we reject the null hypothesis.

When comparing two groups to determine statistical significance, a t-test is a common choice. Indeed, in many situations it is the correct choice. However, another choice exists and should be used in many situations in place of the t-test.

4.2 Parametric vs. Non-Parametric Statistical Tests

If the concept of a p-value is the most misinterpreted in frequentist statsistics, then parametric statistics is a close second. Parametric and non-parametric approaches to determine statistical significance offer two contrasting paradigms. A parametric statistical test is one that makes certain assumptions about the properties of the population distribution from which the data has been drawn. Conversely, a non-parametric test is one that makes no such assumptions. Consider our dataset we saw in Chapter 3, and let's suppose our hypothesis before collecting the data was that male and female patients had different proportions of gMDSC in their circulation. If we wanted to determine whether significant differences exist between the two groups, we may choose to use a t-test.

4.2.1 t-test

Let's start by installing and importing the necessary packages, and then reading in the raw data.

```python
import pandas as pd
import scipy.stats as stats
import numpy as np
import statsmodels.stats.power as sms
from statsmodels.formula.api import ols
from statsmodels.stats.anova import anova_lm
from statsmodels.stats.multicomp import pairwise_tukeyhsd

rawData = pd.read_csv('/Users/yourname/Desktop/datascience/data_science_for_immunologists.csv')
```

```r
install.packages("pwr", dependencies=TRUE)
install.packages("car", dependencies=TRUE)

library("pwr")
library("car")

rawData = read.csv('/Users/yourname/Desktop/datascience/data_science_for_immunologists.csv', header=T, na.strings=c("","NA"))
```

Now we're ready to conduct a t-test. We need to remember to drop any missing values from our data (i.e. where the gender of a participant is unknown or not collected at the time of sampling) first before running the test. Rows with missing values are dropped from the data frame using `.dropna()` in Python and `na.omit` in R.

```python
myData = rawData[['gender','gMDSC']].dropna()
```

```
2   t1 = myData[myData.gender=='M'][ 'gMDSC']
3   t2 = myData[myData.gender=='F'][ 'gMDSC']
4   stats.ttest_ind(t1, t2, equal_var=False).pvalue
```

```
1   myData = na.omit(rawData[,c("gMDSC","gender")])
2   t1 = myData[myData$gender=='M',]$gMDSC
3   t2 = myData[myData$gender=='F',]$gMDSC
4   t.test(t1,t2)
```

This returns a p-value of 0.01. As this is less than the conventional value of 0.05, we conclude that there are significant differences between the two groups.

4.2.2 Mann-Whitney U test

The t-test falls under the category of parametric statistical tests as there are some assumptions on which the calculation of the p-value is based. The critical assumption of the t-test is that each group of data is Gaussian (normally) distributed, and because of this the test statistic (i.e. difference in means) is t-distributed. This assumption gives the t-test its name.

So, continuing the example above, you should hopefully now be questioning whether our data in each group is normally distributed. If it isn't, then we shouldn't be using the t-test, but rather its related cousin - the Mann-Whitney U test. The Mann-Whitney U test makes no assumptions about the data, and as such it is a non-parametric test - calculations are based purely on where each observation ranks when compared to other observations.

Thankfully, there are several methods available to test whether data is normally distributed. The Kolmogorov-Smirnov test is a general statistical test that can be used to assess how well a dataset fits any given specified distribution. The Shapiro-Wilk test specifically tests the null hypothesis that the data is drawn from a normal distribution; if the p-value from this test is less than 0.05, we can conclude that the data is not normally distributed and use the Mann-Whitney U test instead.

```
1   stats.shapiro(myData['gMDSC'])
```

```
shapiro.test(myData$gMDSC)
```

The Shapiro-Wilk test returns a test statistic of 0.89 and a corresponding p-value of 0.0003. Thus, we cannot make the assumption required for a parametric t-test, and should therefore use the non-parametric Mann-Whitney U test. Note that the Mann-Whitney U test is also sometimes called the Wilcoxon rank sum test, and is referred to by this name in R.

```
stats.mannwhitneyu(t1,t2, alternative='two-sided').pvalue
```

```
wilcox.test(t1,t2)
```

Our Mann-Whitney U test gives us a p-value of 0.006, so we have sufficient evidence to reject our null hypothesis and can conclude that there is a difference between males and females where peripheral gMDSC frequencies are concerned.

4.3 How Can We Compare More Than Two Groups?

The t-test and Mann-Whitney test are designed to compare a particular variable between two groups, but sometimes we want to compare more than two groups. Suppose, for example, that rather than comparing the % of gMDSC between males and females, we want to compare % of gMDSC between different disease phases; immunotolerants (IT), immune actives (IA) and inactive low-level carriers (IC). We could proceed by using a t-test or Mann-Whitney U test (depending on whether our data is normally distributed) and conduct three pairwise comparsions between all pairs of groups (i.e. IT vs. IA, IT vs. IC and IA vs. IC). However, this approach raises the possibility of what is known as the 'multiple comparisons problem', where we increase the chance of a Type I error.

A Type I error occurs when the null hypothesis is falsely rejected. In other words, this happens when we conclude that there is enough evidence to reject our null hypothesis, even though it is actually true (i.e. no relationship exists in our data but we conclude that a significant relationship does indeed exist). The reason that multiple hypothesis testing increases our chance of a Type I error can be shown with some simple maths, and comes down to our definition of a p-value.

Recall that if we use a p-value of 0.05, we will only conclude that a significant relationship exists if there was less than a 5% chance of observing our actual data when the null hypothesis is true. Thus, there is a 5% chance that we falsely reject our null hyothesis when it is true. In other words, if there is never any difference in the two groups we are comparing, then 5% of the time we will incorrectly conclude that there is a difference, simply due to the way in which p-values, and more generally frequentist statistics, work.

Now suppose that we test 100 hypothesis tests on a set of data. If each of our null hypotheses was indeed true, then we would incorrectly reject the null hypothesis for 5 of those hypotheses on average, concluding a 'significant' relationship exists 5 times when actually no real relationship exists in any of those cases. Put more bluntly, if each statistical test is independent, this means that the probablity of at least one incorrect rejection of the null hypothesis is

$$1 - 0.95^{100} = 0.994. \tag{4.1}$$

So how do we protect against making this kind of error, and what does this have to do with comparing more than two groups? Well, if we go back to comparing the three groups that we mentioned earlier (IT vs. IA, IT vs. IC and IA vs. IC), it becomes apparent that we run the risk of a Type I error; we're making 3 different comparisons. The chance of a Type I error when making 3 comparisons is

$$1 - 0.95^3 = 0.143. \tag{4.2}$$

Thus, we have approximately a 14% chance of erroneously rejecting one of our three null hypotheses. To guard against this, you may think about reducing our p-value to something less than 0.05. Whilst this temptation is understandable, this actually increases the chance of the other type of error - a Type II error. A Type II error occurs when we incorrectly fail to reject the null hypothesis (i.e. a relationship exists between % gMDSC and disease stage, but our statistical approach fails to give us sufficient sensitivity to detect this relationship).

4.3.1 One-Way ANOVA

Thus, to correctly test whether differences exist between more than two groups of people, we should not be using a *t*-test. Instead, we should use a one-way ANOVA (meaning one-way analysis of variance; we'll come on to two-way ANOVA later on) to compare the means of each group. The key point is that an ANOVA makes sure that we limit our chances of concluding a relationship exists when in reality it doesn't (Type I error), whilst also limiting our chances of concluding that no relationship exists when one does actually exist (Type II error).

Now that the theory is out of the way, let's get to the practical aspect of using an ANOVA.

```
1  myData = rawData[['diseaseClass','gMDSC']].dropna()
2  t1 = myData[myData.diseaseClass=='IC']['gMDSC']
3  t2 = myData[myData.diseaseClass=='IA']['gMDSC']
4  t3 = myData[myData.diseaseClass=='IT']['gMDSC']
5  stats.f_oneway( t1, t2, t3 )
```

```
1  myData = na.omit(rawData[,c("gMDSC","diseaseClass")])
2  anova = aov(gMDSC ~ diseaseClass, data=myData)
3  summary(anova)
```

Our test statistic is 16.5 and corresponding p-value is 0.000004. Thus we conclude that a significant relationship between % gMDSC and disease stage does indeed exist. Remember that we are comparing three groups, so this p-value tells us whether a difference exists between % gMDSC and disease stage, but it does not tell us exactly *which* groups are different. To do this, we would need to use what is known as a post-hoc test, an example being Tukey's Honestly Significant Difference (HSD) test.

```
1  tukey = pairwise_tukeyhsd(endog=myData['gMDSC'], groups=myData['diseaseClass'])
2  tukey.summary()
```

```
1  TukeyHSD(anova)
```

Using Python, check the 'reject' column after running `tukey.summary()` to decide which of the pairwise comparisons are significantly different. Using R, we can look at the 'p adj' column after running `TukeyHSD(anova)` to obtain the p-values for each pairwise comparison. In this example, we should reject each of our null hypotheses, and conclude that significant differences do in fact exist between gMDSC frequencies in all three disease stages. In other words, gMDSC frequencies vary across the course of infection.

Finally, just as choosing between a t-test and a Mann Whitney U test depends on whether the data is normally distributed, we face the same choice when comparing more than two groups. The ANOVA is the parametric extension of the t-test, when we need to compare more than two groups. The non-parametric equivalent of the ANOVA is the Kruskal-Wallis test. Recall that the Shapiro Wilk test we conducted earlier informed us that we should use a non-parametric test, so we should actually use the Kruskal-Wallis test.

```
stats.kruskal(t1,t2,t3)
```

```
kruskal.test(gMDSC ~ diseaseClass, data=myData)
```

Having run the test, this gives us a p-value of 0.00005, and so we conclude that gMDSC frequencies do indeed vary significantly between different disease stages of chronic hepatitis B infection.

4.3.2 Two-Way ANOVA

A one-way ANOVA determines whether one continuous variable significantly changes amongst three or more groups of the same categorical variable. If we are interested in how *two* continuous variables change amongst three or more groups, we need to use the two-way ANOVA.

Let's consider an example where we want to test whether gender and presence/absence of one of the viral antigens, HBeAg, has any effect on an another viral antigen known as HBsAg. Using a two-way ANOVA, we can determine the relationship between gender and HBsAg, and then HBeAg and HBsAg, while controlling for Type

I and Type II errors. Before we look at the code, we need to introduce another concept that must be considered when running an ANOVA. ANOVA calculations can be carried out in three different ways (annoyingly referred to as 'types', just like the types of errors) and can yield different p-values depending on which type is used. The exact nature of the hypothesis that you are testing determines which type of calulcation to use: -

- Type I: This tests the main effect of one factor (e.g. gender), followed by the main effect of the other factor (e.g. the presence/absence of circulating HBeAG) after the main effect of the first factor, followed by the interaction effect between the two factors after their main effects. Note that if gender is considered to be the first factor, and then eAg status the second, different p-values will likely be observed. Thus the order of variables is important for Type I.

- Type II: This tests the effect of one factor after controlling for the other factor, and so the order of first and second factor is irrelevant (i.e. you will obtain the same p-values regardless of whether you choose to test HBeAg as the first or second factor).

- Type III: This tests the effect of one factor after controlling for the other factor *and* the interaction between the two factors. As with Type II tests, you will obtain the same p-values regardless of whether you choose HBeAg as the first or second factor.

The type of test you choose should depend on what assumption you are making about your model. Usually the hypothesis of interest concerns the effect of one factor while controlling for the other, meaning Types II or III are usually preferred. Let's start by considering an example where we are not interested in controlling for the interaction between gender and eAg, so we will use Type II in the following example.

```
myData = rawData[['sAg','gender','eAg']].dropna()
model = ols('sAg ~ gender + eAg', myData).fit()
aov_table = anova_lm(model, typ=2)
aov_table
```

```
myData = na.omit(rawData[,c("sAg","eAg","gender")])
twoway_anova = aov( sAg ~ gender * eAg, data=myData)
Anova(twoway_anova, type = "II")
```

Looking at the p-values in the last column (labeled $Pr(>F)$), we can see that no significant relationship exists between either independent variable. You should obtain p-values of 0.34 and 0.20 for gender vs. HBsAg and HBeAg vs. HBsAg respectively, and 0.09 for the interaction between gender and HBeAg.

4.4 Correlation vs. Regression

The t-test we used above told us that gMDSC frequencies are significantly different in male and female patients with hepatitis B infection. In that instance, we were comparing one categorical group (males vs. females) against a continuous *response* variable. However, in some situations, we want to assess the relationship between two continuous variables, which we will call Y and X for convenience. The two most common approaches that exist to quantify this are correlation and regression, but there often seems to be confusion over which to use and when.

Linear regression [26] tells us more about the relationship between two (continuous) variables than Pearson's correlation coefficient. Using linear regression, we obtain the following pieces of information:-

1. The 'slope' of the straight line that best fits the relationship between your two chosen variables, which tells you how much Y will change given one unit increase in X.

2. The 'intercept' of the straight line that best fits the relationship between your two chosen variables, which tells us what the value of Y is when $X=0$.

3. A quantification of how well this line fits the data. This is the so-called R^2 value, which is nearer 0 when the line is not a good fit and nearer 1 when it is a good fit.

4. A predictive model which gives us the most likely value of Y for a given of X.

Pearson's correlation coefficient gives only the sign of the 'slope' (but not the value of it). Furthermore, it does not give the intercept or a method by which we can predict the value of Y in the future based on the value of X. Instead, all it gives us is the quantification of how much one variable might change when the other variable changes.

Based on these facts, you may assume that linear regression is always best to use as it gives us more information about our data. However, regression is inappropriate to use when we have no reason to believe that the value of one variable is a response to the value of the other variable; correlation would be more appropriate to use in such scenarios.

Consider the two continuous variables in our dataset called *white_cell_count_per_litre* and *gMDSC*, and consider Pearson's correlation coefficient initially. We can calculate Pearson's correlation coefficient using the following code.

```
1  myData = rawData[['white_cell_count_per_litre','gMDSC']].dropna()
2  stats.pearsonr(myData['white_cell_count_per_litre'],myData['gMDSC'])
```

```
1  myData = na.omit(rawData[,c("gMDSC","white_cell_count_per_litre")])
2  cor(myData$white_cell_count_per_litre,myData$gMDSC, method='pearson')
```

This gives us a correlation coefficient of 0.19, implying moderate correlation. Coefficients close to 1 or -1 indicate a strong, positive and strong, negative relationship respectively. It is important to point out that Pearson's correlation coefficient is designed to detect only linear relationships between two variables. An alternative exists that can detect any monotonically increasing relationship, that is a relationship where the slope of the imaginary line that best fits the two variables is always of the same sign, but may change value. Contrast this to Pearson's correlation coefficient, where this imaginary line is the same sign and the same value at all points on the line (Figure 4.1).

As the name suggests, Spearman's rank correlation coefficient is based on ranking each variable according to how it compares to other values of that variable in the sample of data. This is why it is able to detect non-linear relationships as well as those that are linear. Care should be taken when choosing between these two measures of correlation; the selection should be based on the nature of the relationship you want to detect. Figure 4.1 shows the difference between a linear

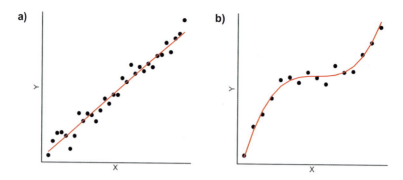

Figure 4.1: Example scatterplots depicting **a** data with a linear relationship between variables (X and Y), where a proportional increase in the dependent variable (y-axis) will be observed for every unit increase in the independent variable (x-axis), and **b** data with a monotonically increasing relationship where the dependent variable (y-axis) will always increase for a unit increase in the independent variable (x-axis) but not necessarily in a proportion manner. The red lines on both plots represent the hypothetical lines of best fit.

relationship and a non-linear monotonically increasing relationship.

We can determine Spearman's rank correlation coefficient using the following code:

```
myData = rawData[['white_cell_count_per_litre','gMDSC']].dropna()
stats.spearmanr(myData['white_cell_count_per_litre'],myData['gMDSC'])
```

```
myData = na.omit(rawData[,c("gMDSC","white_cell_count_per_litre")])
cor(myData$white_cell_count_per_litre,myData$gMDSC, method='spearman')
```

Thus, Spearman's rank correlation coefficient gives us a very similar value of 0.17, representing a slight positive correlation between our two variables.

In this instance, correlation would be the correct choice over regression as we have no prior hypothesis that one variable changes in response to the other. To illustrate an example of how to fit a linear regression model, let's consider an alternative situation where we are interested in the relationship between *ALT* (a clinical measure of liver damage) and *gMDSC*. In this instance, linear regression would seem a more appropriate choice as ALT might resonably be considered a 'response' to gMDSC frequencies in patients. Thus, our *X* variable (the variable being used to predict) would be *gMDSC* and our *Y* variable (the variable that responds to the predictor variable) is ALT.

We can fit a linear regression model to this data using the following code.

```
1  myData = rawData[['gMDSC','alt']].dropna()
2  stats.linregress(myData['gMDSC'],myData['alt'])
```

```
1  myData = na.omit(rawData[,c("gMDSC","alt")])
2  linear_regression = lm( alt ~ gMDSC, data=myData)
3  linear_regression
```

Remember how linear regression gives us more information than the correlation between two variables. Using linear regression, we also find that the 'slope' is -1.29 and 'intercept' is 70.3. Far from abstract quantities, both of these values tell us something useful about the relationship between the two variables. The slope tells us that for every unit increase in gMDSC frequencies in patients (i.e. for every percentage point increase in gMDSC frequencies), the patient's ALT decreases by 1.29 IU/L. Moreover, the intercept tells us that the best estimate for ALT when a patient has no gMDSC is 70.3 IU/L. Of course care must be taken when interpreting these values, as they may not always have an obviously interpretable meaning if gMDSC frequencies never reach zero in any patient. However, we can reasonably conclude that gMDSC reflect a means of reducing liver inflammation in the context of HBV infection.

4.5 Chi-squared Test

Sometimes the variables we want to compare are not on a continuous scale, but rather are categorical. This means that we cannot use the statistical tests outlined above, as they are designed for use only with continuous variables.

We saw earlier in this Chapter that males and females have different gMDSC frequencies. In this scenario, gender is a categorical variable that takes two values (M or F) and gMDSC frequencies are continuous. Given that we found that significant differences exist between gMDSC frequencies according to gender, it seems reasonable to hypothesise that disease stage and gender may also be dependent on each other. Our null hypothesis would be that disease stage is independent of gender, while our alternative hypothesis would be that the two are related. For example, we may hypothesise that higher gMDSC frequencies in females may result in less inflammation, meaning female patients may be more likely to have 'inactive' disease and be clinically assigned as a low-level carrier.

To test this hypothesis, we require a chi-squared (χ^2) test. The chi-squared test first calculates the expected frequencies for each combination of categorical variables, and then compares the observed frequencies to the expected frequencies to determine whether they are significantly different. Expected frequencies are determined using what are called the marginal probabilities - the probability of a given variable without taking into account any other variables. To understand this more easily, let's count the frequencies in each combination of categories.

```
myData = rawData[['diseaseClass','gender']].dropna()
counts = pd.crosstab( myData.gender, myData.diseaseClass)
counts
```

```
myData = na.omit(rawData[,c("diseaseClass","gender")])
counts = table(myData)
counts
```

The table called `counts` is known as the contingency table, and it shows the number of patients that lie in each categorical combination. For example, there are 13 male inactives in our sample, 5 female immunocompetents and so on. We can get the expected frequencies in each cell in the table by multiplying the proportion of observations we have for one of the categorical variables with the count of the other variable. For example, the expected number of inactive males in our sample is

$$E(IA, M) = P(IA) \times Count(M) = P(M) \times Count(IA) \qquad (4.3)$$

where *P(IA)* is the proportion of inactive patients in our sample and *Count(M)* is the number of males in our sample. Performing this calculation for each combination of categories in turn gives us the following table

	IA	IC	IT
F	4.6	6.2	4.2
M	9.4	12.8	8.8

The chi-squared test statistic is simply calculated using

$$\frac{(Observed - Expected)^2}{Expected}, \qquad (4.4)$$

and summing these values up over all the cells in the table, and then comparing to a reference table to determine what the associated p-value is. Fortunately, we can use built-in functions that perform these steps for us, and so we can determine the p-value from the chi-squared test simply by using the following code.

```
print("p-value =",stats.chi2_contingency(counts)[1])
```

```
chi_test = chisq.test(myData$gender, myData$diseaseClass)
chi_test
```

Thus, our p-value of 0.002 tells us we can reject the null hypothesis and conclude that disease stage and gender are indeed related. This should not come as too much of a surprise when we look at the actual counts for males and females in each disease phase in our dataset.

	IA	IC	IT
F	1	5	9
M	13	14	4

4.6 Power Calculations

Power calculations form an important part in informing the design of an experiment. The above statistical tests are used after data has been collected, to test our hypotheses and draw scientific conclusions from the data. Power calculations are performed before data is collected, typically to determine how big the sample should be.

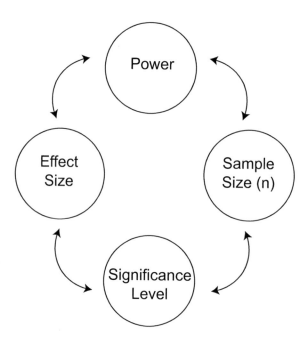

Figure 4.2: Schematic to show that the relationship between power, effect size, sample size and significance level are all interlinked; to calculate one value you will need to know the values of each of the other parameters.

In most situations, we want to know how big the sample needs to be to detect a relationship of a given size. For example, suppose our interest had been piqued in a potential relationship that may exist between gender and HBV viral load. In this case, our null hypothesis is 'there is no difference in viral load between men and women'. To either reject or accept this null hypothesis, we will need to collect some data by sampling a group of men and a group of women from the whole population, the question is how many people in each group do we need to recruit to our study?

To understand how we calculate the most suitable number of people to recruit, it is important to understand the relationship between the size of a sample, the power of the hypothesis test, the effect size and the significance crtierion used for the hypothesis test.

There are several new terms here, so let's first define each of them.

- **Power:** The power of a hypothesis test is the probability of rejecting the null hypothesis when it is false. In other words, it is our ability to detect a relationship between gender and viral load in our sample if a relationship does indeed exist.

- **Effect Size:** The difference between the two groups under consideration.
- **Significance criterion:** The level at which we would consider our observed data to be unlikely to have occurred by chance, leading us to reject the null hypothesis. In other words, the p-value we intend to use to test whether we should reject the null hypothesis.
- **Sample size:** The number of observations that are collected, and which are used to decide whether to reject the null hypothesis.

In a typical scenario, we want to calculate how big our sample should be to give us sufficient power to reject our null hypothesis if it is false. In other words, how many observations do we need to make in order to find a difference if there is one. In general, the larger the power, the smaller the effect size and the smaller the significance criterion will all result in requiring a larger sample size. Conversely, the smaller the power, the larger the effect size and the larger the significance criterion will all result in requiring a smaller sample size.

This will hopefully feel intuitive. If we plan on using a p-value of 0.01, we are being more stringent when deciding whether to reject the null hypothesis. By convention, we use a power $1 - \alpha = 0.8$ and a significance criterion (p-value) of 0.05. The effect size would either need to be estimated based on prior knowledge, or else it could be determined by using preliminary data from a previous study.

To provide an example of how we would calculate efffect size from a preliminary dataset, suppose that the dataset we have been using in our examples above is a preliminary dataset on which we wish to base a sample size calculation.. Returning to our example mentioned earlier, suppose our null hypothesis is 'there is no difference in white blood cell counts between men and women'. In this case, we would want to understand the effect size in white blood cell counts between men and women. We can do this using the code below.

```
myData = rawData[['white_cell_count_per_litre','gender']].dropna()
mean_males = myData[myData.gender=='M']['white_cell_count_per_litre'].mean()
mean_females = myData[myData.gender=='F']['white_cell_count_per_litre'].mean()
standard_deviation = myData['white_cell_count_per_litre'].std()
effect_size = (mean_females - mean_males) / standard_deviation
```

```
6  print(effect_size)
```

```
1  myData = na.omit(rawData[,c("white_cell_count_per_litre","gender")])
2  mean_males = mean(myData[myData$gender=='M',]$white_cell_count_per_litre)
3  mean_females = mean(myData[myData$gender=='F',]$white_cell_count_per_litre)
4  standard_deviation = sd(myData$white_cell_count_per_litre)
5  effect_size = (mean_females - mean_males) / standard_deviation
6  effect_size
```

This gives us an effect size of 0.46, which we can use to determine how big our sample size should be using the following code.

```
1  sms.tt_ind_solve_power(effect_size=effect_size, alpha=0.05, power=0.8, alternative='two-sided')
```

```
1  power.t.test( d=effect_size, sig.level=0.05, power=0.8)
```

Thus, based on the effect size we have observed in this 'preliminary' data, we would conclude that 75 people are needed in each group (i.e. 75 men and 75 women) to find a signifcant relationship if one does indeed exist.

Chapter 5

Clustering

5.1 What is Clustering?

Putting observations into groups based on shared attributes is a common task in many fields. Specifically in immunuology, perhaps the most common application of grouping similar objects together is in flow cytometry, where the primary aim is to group cells based on shared marker expression profiles. Likewise, we may also want to group patients together based on equivalent clinical attributes to determine a treatment plan. A data-driven approach should be used to decide which patients belong to which group, to ensure that the groups best reflect shared characteristics.

Groups of observations/events/patients are usually referred to as clusters. Typically, however, the underlying truth is rarely known, which means we do not know what the 'correct' clusters should look like. We could find several different ways in which to group our data, all of which may be meaningful. This may seem at first paradoxical, but it's actually a common problem, so much so that it constitutes an area of machine learning in its own right called **unsupervised learning**. Unsupervised learning covers the set of problems where we do not actually know what the underlying truth is, but rather we are looking to find some underlying structure to make sense of our data.

Due to the fact that clustering is generally carried out in an unsupervised manner, two questions arise as a consequence:-

- Which features (variables) should I base my clusters on?

- How many clusters exist within the data?

Note that up to this point we have used the word data very generally when talking about clustering 'data'. Of course, in reality, we have a dataset that may contain many features which we have measured experimentally. We may decide which of these features to use for clustering in a mathematical way or in a hypothesis-driven way. Using a mathematical approach, we might look to include those features which are most different across the data (i.e those with the largest variance) or those features which give us the tightest clusters (i.e. minimise the silhouette of the clusters - we will discuss silhouettes in more detail later in the chapter, but for now can be thought of as a measure of how distinct each group is from each other). In a hypothesis-driven approach, we might look to include only those features which we believe to have an effect on the target of the clustering (i.e. we may hypothesise that activated HLA-DR+ (or CD38+) CD4+ T cells may have different functions to non-activated, resting HLA-DR-CD4+ T cells, in which case we would of course deliberately choose to cluster on HLA-DR (or CD38) and CD4).

The key point to emphasise when clustering is that different inputs give different outputs. In other words, the features you choose as inputs will naturally have a large effect on the clusters you find, so choose wisely!

5.2 Centroid-Driven Clusters: K-Means Clustering

Perhaps the most widely used algorithm to extract meaning from a dataset by identifying clusters is the K-means algorithm [27]. Briefly, this algorithm works on the premise that you, the scientist, tell the algorithm how many clusters (K) you are looking for, and the algorithm then finds the best way to split the data into K clusters. In reality, you will often not know how many clusters you expect to find, due to it being an unsupervised approach, but we will come back to this point later. The algorithm works as follows: -

1. Start with a random set of K 'centroids' (where K is the number of clusters you are looking to find) where each K represents the central point of every cluster

2. Assign each observation to the cluster represented by the nearest *K* based on distance.

3. Find the centroid of these clusters and repeat step 2 for many iterations.

Thus, K-means clustering is an iterative algorithm that starts randomly and converges to an appropriate solution, where each observation is assigned to its nearest centroid. There are many alternatives closely related to this approach (K-medoids, K-prototypes) as well as a whole host of other algorithms using distinct approaches to the iterative process described above.

For now, let's focus solely on the K-means algorithm and for the time being let's imagine that we know we are looking for 2 clusters (so *K=2*). We start by importing all the relevant packages we will need for the code in this chapter.

```python
import pandas as pd
import scipy.stats as stats
import numpy as np
import seaborn as sns

from sklearn.cluster import KMeans, AgglomerativeClustering, DBSCAN
from sklearn.mixture import GaussianMixture
from sklearn.metrics import silhouette_score, adjusted_rand_score
from sklearn.preprocessing import scale

import matplotlib.pyplot as plt

%matplotlib inline
sns.set(style='ticks',font_scale=1.5)
```

```r
install.packages("fpc", dependencies = TRUE)
install.packages("GGally", dependencies = TRUE)
install.packages("mclust", dependencies = TRUE)
install.packages("cluster", dependencies = TRUE)

library(fpc)
library(GGally)
library(mclust)
library(cluster)
```

Next we will need to read in the data, and we will continue to use the same dataset we've used throughout the book so far. Once we have imported the data, we need to decide which inputs we will use to determine our clusters. As an example, let's suppose we want to cluster patients using three features - HBV viral load, age and sAg. Although many cases for clustering are unsupervised, for the purpose of this example let's suppose that we know the underlying truth for each observation, making this a supervised learning task.

Thus, we define X to be the input data frame for clustering, and it contains the three features we are interested in basing our clustering on.

```
1  rawData = pd.read_csv('/Users/yourname/Desktop/datascience/data_science_for_
       immunologists.csv')
2  features = ['viralLoad','age','sAg']
```

```
1  rawData = read.csv('/Users/yourname/Desktop/datascience/data_science_for_
       immunologists.csv', header=T, na.strings=c("","NA"))
2  features = c('viralLoad','age','sAg')
```

The cluster each patient is put in is based on whichever cluster centroid they are nearest to. Once we have run the K-means algorithm and found the cluster centres, the cluster labels for each patient can be easily determined. To start with, we need to scale the data and run the K-means algorithm.

```
1  myData = rawData[features+['eAg']].dropna().reset_index().drop('index',axis=1)
2  X = scale(myData[features])
3  kmeans = KMeans(n_clusters=2, random_state=0).fit(X)
```

```
1  myData = na.omit(rawData[,c(features,"eAg")])
2  X = scale(myData[,features], center = TRUE, scale = TRUE)
3  kmeans_clustering = kmeans( X, 2)
```

In both the Python and R code, each line is performing the same task. As usual, we include the code in line 1 to drop any missing values from the data frame. Line 2 scales the data and finally line 3 performs the K-means algorithm. Once we have run the algorithm, we need to generate a new column in our data frame to store the results of the clustering algorithm, before finally visualising the results to observe how the data has been clustered.

```
1  myData = myData.assign(kmeans_labels = pd.Series(kmeans.labels_).values)
2  centres = kmeans.cluster_centers_
3  centres
4  g = sns.pairplot(data=myData, vars=features, hue='kmeans_labels', diag_kind='kde')
```

```
1  myData$clusters = kmeans_clustering$cluster
2  centres = kmeans_clustering$centers
3  centres
4  myData$clusters <- as.factor(myData$clusters)
5  ggpairs(data=myData[,c(features,'clusters')], mapping=ggplot2::aes(colour =
       clusters))
```

Line 1 generates a new column in the data frame that labels each observation according to which cluster it has been assigned. Lines 2 and 3 can be used to determine the centre of each cluster if required, although this is of course optional. Finally, line 4 (in Python, lines 4 and 5 in R) allows us to visualise the results (Figure 5.1), and is perhaps the most important part of the clustering process. In this example, we only based our clusters on three features, and so visualisation is straightforward. However, when we have more than two or three features, visualisation of data becomes more difficult. This is an important distinction, and we will return to dealing with such a scenario later in this chapter. For the time being, let's visualise the clusters we've found using two features. The beauty of writing your own code to do this lies in your ability to customise your plots however you want. In this example, each point represents a different patient, and so let's colour each point according to which cluster the K-means algorithm placed the patient in.

5.2.1 Assessing the Quality of the Clusters

Assessing the quality of the clusters that we have found depends on whether we are carrying out a supervised or unsupervised clustering task. In a supervised task,

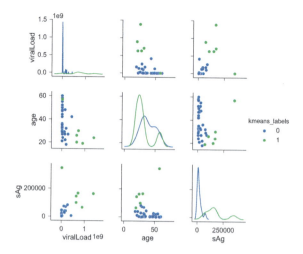

Figure 5.1: Figure represents the output of the K-means clustering algorithm. Each subfigure represents the pairwise relationship across each variable on which the clustering is based. K-means clustering was used to identify two clusters of patients. The data points are coloured blue and green according to which cluster they belong.

such as the previous example, the quality of our clustering can be calculated with relative ease. In this scenario, we are trying to get some sense of the 'accuracy' of the clusters (see Chapter 7 for various means by which we can judge accuracy). The Rand index is often used to assess cluster quality, and gives an easy-to-understand measure of how well observations have been grouped together. In our example, we want to group all patients who are HBeAg+ in one cluster, and all patients who are HBeAg- in another cluster. We have a dataset consisting of 40 patients. We now have two different labels for each patient - the 'actual' label that tells us whether the patient really is HBeAg+, and the 'cluster' label that the K-means algorithm has assigned to each patient. The Rand index is defined as

$$R = \frac{a+b}{a+b+c+d} \quad (5.1)$$

where

a = the number of observations that have the same actual label AND the same cluster label

b = the number of observations that have the same actual label AND a different cluster label

c = the number of observations that have a different actual label AND the same cluster label

d = the number of observations that have a different actual label AND a different cluster label

However, we can do slightly better than this measure using the adjusted Rand index. The adjusted Rand index is similar to the Rand index, but accounts for the fact that some cluster labels will match purely by chance. Recall Chapter 4 where we looked at how rigorous statistical testing should always account for how likely something is to occur purely by chance.

$$AdjustedR = \frac{R - ExpectedR}{MaxR - ExpectedR} \qquad (5.2)$$

This gives a measure that varies between -1 and 1. When the clusters we find perfectly match the actual labels, we get an adjusted Rand index of 1, and when the clusters are no better than random, we get an index of 0. To calculate the adjusted R index, we use the following code: -

```
1  actuals = myData['eAg']
2  adjusted_rand_score(actuals, kmeans.labels_)
```

```
1  actuals = unlist(lapply(myData$eAg, as.integer))
2  adjustedRandIndex(actuals, myData$clusters)
```

This gives us an adjusted Rand index of 0.09, indicating that our clustering is not particularly successful in grouping patients by the presence of absence of the viral antigen HBeAg. To improve this, we could adopt one or more of the following strategies:-

- Use different/more features to cluster patients.
- Use a different technique to perform the clustering.

Let's consider the second point.

5.3 Linkage-Driven Clustering: Hierarchical Clustering

K-means clustering is perhaps the most ubiquitous method for clustering, largely thanks to its intuitive, easy-to-understand method. However, there are of course many other algorithms that can be used to ultimately reach the same goal - that is, labeling every observation according to which group it is deemed to belong.

Another very popular method is hierarchical clustering, which relies on the notion of distance between observations to group them together. The first step in the algorithm is to calculate the distances between each pair of points. Typically Euclidean distance is used, which is a technical way of saying the intuitive distance between data points (it is mathemtaically the square root of the sum of square differences). This is colloquially often referred to as the distance 'as the crow flies'.

Hierarchical clustering is an iterative algorithm that consists of two steps at each iteration. Observations are grouped together to make successively larger or smaller groups, depending on whether the clustering is done is an agglomerative (bottom-up) or divisive (top-down) manner. If we consider the bottom-up approach, we would start with each of our observations representing a separate cluster. We would then group the two observations together that are most similar (in terms of nearest distance). We then re-calculate all distances between observations, but note that the distance from each of the remaining observations to the 'cluster' containing two observations will be calculated slightly differently. In this case, it will either be calculated using the distance from the individual observation to the mean of the 'cluster', or by using the maximum distance between the individual observation and each of the observations within the 'cluster', or by using the minimum distance between the individual observation and each of the observations within the 'cluster'. These approaches are usually referred to as average-linkage, complete-linkage or minimum-linkage, and the same approach must be used at each iteration.

This process is repeated until finally all observations lie in the same cluster. Using this approach, it is possible to get a clustering at each level, in other words at each iteration the total number of clusters will be one less than the previous iteration. Again, as a data scientist we must define how many clusters we wish to find, after which it is simply a case of choosing the appropriate level in the hierarchy that gives us this number of clusters.

Let's now consider how hierarchical clustering compares to K-means clustering. Again we will use HBV viral load, HBsAg and age as our features, and our hypothesis is that patients will group together based on these three features, according to whether they are HBeAg positive or negative. For this reason, we again need to set the number of clusters we want to find to be equal to two, and we will now use hierarchical clustering to group our patients. Once we've performed the clustering, we can again determine which cluster each patient belongs to, and plot the results in the same way we did before (Figure 5.2).

```
1  myData = rawData[features+['eAg']].dropna().reset_index().drop('index',axis=1)
2  X = scale(myData[features])
3  agg_clustering = AgglomerativeClustering(n_clusters=2).fit(X)
4
5  myData = myData.assign(agg_clustering_labels = pd.Series(agg_clustering.labels_).values)
6
7  g = sns.pairplot(data=myData, vars=features, hue='agg_clustering_labels', diag_kind='kde')
```

```
1  myData = na.omit(rawData[,c(features,"eAg")])
2  X = scale(myData[,features], center = TRUE, scale = TRUE)
3  calculate_hc = hclust(dist(X), method='complete')
4  hierarchical_clustering = cutree(calculate_hc, 2)
5
6  myData$clusters = hierarchical_clustering
7
8  myData$clusters <- as.factor(myData$clusters)
9  ggpairs(data=myData[,c(features,'clusters')], mapping=ggplot2::aes(colour = clusters))
```

Qualitatively, we can see that the patients have been clustered in exactly the same way as they were using the K-means algorithm. We can confirm this by checking the Rand index,

```
1  actuals = myData['eAg']
2  adjusted_rand_score(actuals, agg_clustering.labels_)
```

```
actuals = unlist(lapply(myData$eAg, as.integer))
adjustedRandIndex(actuals, myData$clusters)
```

and finally by counting what proportion of assigned group labels are the same when using both methods of clustering.

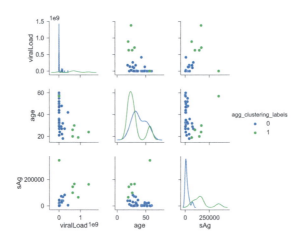

Figure 5.2: Figure represents the output of the hierarchical clustering algorithm. Each subfigure represents the pairwise relationship across each variable on which the clustering is based. Hierarchical clustering has been used to identify two clusters of patients. The data points are coloured blue and green according to which cluster they belong.

5.4 Density-driven Clustering: DBSCAN

Similar to hierarchical clustering, in that it uses a distance based threshold when deciding whether to group observations together, density-based spatial clustering of applications with noise (DBSCAN) is a density-based method built on the premise that three types of observations exist: a core point, a reachable point and an outlier [28].

- Core point: an observation is a core point q if at least m points (including the point itself) are within a distance of ϵ. Each of these m observations are called *directly reachable* points from the core point q.

- Reachable point: a point p is reachable if there is a path to it from another core point. A reachable point may also be a core point.

- Outliers: all points that are not reachable or core points are defined as outliers.

The algorithm works by first selecting a random point, and determining whether it is an *outlier* (because less than *m-1* lie within a distance of ϵ) or a core point. If the point is deemed to be an outlier (note that this point may later be found to be a reachable point even if not a core point), then another point is randomly selected until a core point is found. Once a core point q_1 is found, the cluster is started, and all reachable points from q_1 are added to the cluster. Each of these points that are added are then each assesed in turn, and all points within a distance of ϵ to each of these points are added to the cluster. This process continues until no more points can be added to the cluster. When no more points can be added, a new point is randomly chosen and the same process applied until no more points in the data set remain.

Let's look at the code. By now it is hopefully becoming clear that it's quite easy in Python to replace one cluster method with another, as it's only one line that needs to change.

```python
myData = rawData[features+['eAg']].dropna().reset_index().drop('index',axis=1)
X = scale(myData[features])
dbscan = DBSCAN(eps=0.5, min_samples=4).fit(X)

myData = myData.assign(dbscan = pd.Series(dbscan.labels_).values)
g = sns.pairplot(data=myData, vars=features, hue='dbscan', diag_kind='kde')
plt.show()
```

```r
myData = na.omit(rawData[,c(features,"eAg")])
X = scale(myData[,features], center = TRUE, scale = TRUE)

dbscan_clustering = dbscan(X, eps=0.5, MinPts = 4, scale = FALSE, method = "raw",
    seeds = TRUE)
myData$clusters = predict(dbscan_clustering, data=X)

myData$clusters <- as.factor(myData$clusters)
ggpairs(data=myData[,c(features,'clusters')], mapping=ggplot2::aes(colour =
    clusters))
```

We have chosen to run DBSCAN with $\epsilon = 0.5$ and $m = 4$. Recall that clustering is typically done in an unsupervised approach, and choosing the best value for these parameters is not easy to do in a data-driven way. Sometimes it is best to try a number of different values and see what looks best, although this can be hard to do with high dimensional data. The last section in this chapter looks at how to decide what the best values are for a clustering algorithm in a data-driven manner.

We can now see that the clusters generated from DBSCAN are very different to our previous two methods (Figure 5.3). This is becuase DBSCAN is a density-driven approach, and has found a cluster in a particularly dense region of the dataset. This is most obvious when looking at HBV viral load vs. HBsAg, where a dense cluster has been found in the bottom left corner of the plot. Note that if we had chosen different values for ϵ and m, we may well have found different clusters, highlighting how dependent clustering methods are on the chosen parameter values.

Finally, we can check the Rand score to see if our clusters reflect the presence or absence of HBeAg in patients.

```
actuals = myData['eAg']
adjusted_rand_score(actuals, dbscan.labels_)
```

```
actuals = unlist(lapply(myData$eAg, as.integer))
adjustedRandIndex(actuals, myData$clusters)
```

The adjusted Rand index of 0.23 means that a modest amount of overlap exists between the clusters we have found and *eAg* status - the difference in this Rand index to that obtained using the previous approaches highlights how the choice of clustering technique can have a big effect on the groups of patients we find.

5.5 Distribution-driven Clustering: Gaussian Mixture Models

The last paradigm of clustering we will look at is that of distribution-based models, of which Gaussian mixture models (GMM) are the most popular. As the name suggests, the approach assumes that each observation in the dataset is generated

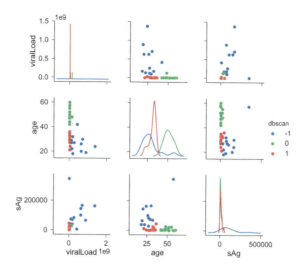

Figure 5.3: Figure represents the output of the DBSCAN clustering algorithm. Each subfigure represents the pairwise relationship across each variable on which the clustering is based. DBSCAN clustering has identified three clusters of patients (based on the chosen algorithm values). The data points are coloured blue, red and green according to which cluster they belong.

by a mixture of Gaussian (normal) distributions. For example, we may want to simply cluster observations based only on HBV viral load, and our hypothesis may be that HBV viral load is dependent on gender. In such a case, we would hypothesise that the data we have for viral load consists of two mixed distributions, one for men and the other for women. The distribution of HBV viral load values in our patients that we would then observe a mixture of the two of these component distributions.

The concept of GMM is fairly straightforward, and again we must supply the number of clusters (sometimes referred to as components) they wish to find. Unlike the concept, the technique required to determine what each of the components looks like is a complex one, called expectation maximisation, and is not something we will look at in any detail in this book.

Let's take a look at the code.

```
myData = rawData[features+['eAg']].dropna().reset_index().drop('index',axis=1)
X = scale(myData[features])
gmm = GaussianMixture(n_components=2).fit(X)
```

```
4
5  myData = myData.assign(gmm = pd.Series(gmm.predict(X)).values)
6  g = sns.pairplot(data=myData, vars=features, hue='gmm', diag_kind='kde')
7  plt.show()
```

```
1  myData = na.omit(rawData[,c(features,"eAg")])
2  X = scale(myData[,features], center = TRUE, scale = TRUE)
3
4  gmm_clustering <- Mclust(X, 2)
5  myData$clusters = gmm_clustering$classification
6
7  myData$clusters <- as.factor(myData$clusters)
8  ggpairs(data=myData[,c(features,'clusters')], mapping=ggplot2::aes(colour =
       clusters))
```

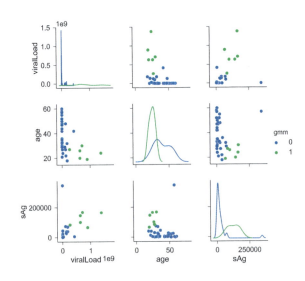

Figure 5.4: Figure represents the output of the Gaussian mixture model (GMM) algorithm. Each subfigure represents the pairwise relationship across each variable on which the clustering is based. GMM was used to identify two clusters of patients. The data points are coloured blue and green according to which cluster they belong.

5.6 How to Choose the Correct Number of Clusters?

So far, once we have grouped patients into clusters using our chosen technique, we have determined how well the patients have been grouped together by comparing the cluster labels given to each patient to the actual label (i.e. presence or absence of the viral protein HBeAg) using the Rand index. However, in most cases where we use clustering, we do not typically know what the groups *should* be - rather we are looking to find some structure in the data that is not immediately apparent. In such cases, we cannot use the Rand index to determine how well the data has been clustered.

The silhouette score provides a measure of how well the data has been grouped together in instances where we do not know the actual labels. When clustering, we are essentially looking for sets of tightly packed groups of observations that are similar to each other within the same cluster, but different to observations in other clusters. This is what the silhoutte score measures - the intra-cluster distance relative to the inter-cluster distance.

For example, in Figure 5.5, we can see the silhouette score for two different sets of (artificial) data. In Figure 5.5a, we can intuitively see that the data splits nicely into 3 distinct clusters. This is reflected in a large silhouette score of 0.83. In Figure 5.5b, we can see that the data less obviously splits into groups, and so the silhouette score is lower; equal to 0.18. A silhouette score can be between -1 and 1. A score of 1 represents a perfect clustering, while 0 means that, on average, each observation is as similar to another cluster as it is to its own. A score less than 0 means that, on average, each observation is more similar to another cluster than it is to its own cluster.

The benefit of using the silhouette after you have clustered a set of observations is that you can use it to determine whether you have chosen the correct number of clusters. The following code allows you to use K-means clustering searching for any number of clusters between two and ten. You can then choose the number of clusters that best fits the data by printing the value of the silhouette score for each value of K.

```
for i in range(2,10):
    myData = rawData[features+['eAg']].dropna().reset_index().drop('index',axis=1)
```

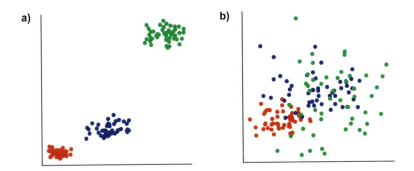

Figure 5.5: Hypothetical data plotted to illustrate silhouette scores by comparing intra-cluster distances with inter-cluster distances. Data shown in **a)** falls into three well-defined clusters, giving a silhouette score of 0.83 (close to 1), whereas data shown in **b)** does not fall into well-defined clusters and consequently its associated silhouette score is 0.18 (closer to zero).

```
3    X = scale(myData[features])
4    kmeans = KMeans(n_clusters=i, random_state=0).fit(X)
5    score = silhouette_score(X, kmeans.labels_)
6    print('Silhouette for {} clusters : {:.2f}'.format(i,score))
```

```
1    for (i in c(2:10)){
2    myData = na.omit(rawData[,c(features,"eAg")])
3    X = scale(myData[,features], center = TRUE, scale = TRUE)
4    kmeans_clustering = kmeans( X, i)
5    silhouette_score = mean(silhouette(kmeans_clustering$cluster, dist(X))[,3])
6    print(paste('Silhouette for ',i,'clusters =',silhouette_score))
7    }
```

Thus, we should group our observations into 2 clusters, as this is the value of K that maximises the silhouette.

5.7 Which Clustering Method Should I Use?

Whilst it would be admirable for any beginner to want to code their own clustering algorithm from scratch, this is usually not necessary thanks to the comprehensive packages that exist in both Python and R. Thus, for the beginner data scientist I would recommend using clustering methods that have already been developed and available to use. Even working within these confines, almost every popular clustering algortihm is available in at least one of the programming languages.

Choosing the 'correct' method is not straightforward - different clustering methods will work well in different scenarios. K-means, for example, implicitly assumes that clusters are convex (spherical), so would not be the best method to use if you expect data points to lie along a long, narrow cylinder. In such cicurmstances, DBSCAN may be more appropriate due to its density-based methodology for discovering clusters. Similarly, for a very large dataset, mixture models do not scale particularly well, and you may be better off using scalable methods like hierarchical clustering.

Ultimately, there is no strict set of rules to guide exactly which method should be used in each situation. Due to the typically unsupervised nature of clustering, it is advisable simply to try several methods and assess the output of each. In situations where your data set has too many variables to easily view graphically, dimension reduction techniques can be used to visualise your high dimensional data and assess the output, and such techniques are where we turn our attention to next.

Chapter 6

Dimension Reduction

6.1 The Shrewd Photographer

At first sight, some definitions of dimension reduction can leave you unable to see the purpose of why such a technique would exist. To help with this, imagine a 'real-life' example where we want to sell our car. We will probably want to write a description of the car, perhaps including its age, colour, make and model. We'll then take some pictures to both faithfully represent what the car looks like as well as trying our best to make it look as good as possible with the primary goal of making more money. Our car has three dimensions, namely its width, length and height. Thus, if we are limited to trying to sell our car using only one photo (in a small advert online perhaps), then we would be faced with a decision, due to the fact that we are trying to represent a 3D object in 2D space. Do we show a photo of only the front of the car (and in doing so show the width and height of the car), only the side of the car (and in doing so show the length and height of the car) or only the top of the car (and in doing so show the width and length of the car)? Hopefully no-one would decide to show a photo only of the top of the car here - which would leave us choosing between showing the front (width and height) or the side of the car (width and length).

However, a shrewd photographer may realise that neither of these two options offer the best view of the car, as they leave out a lot of detail about what the side of the car looks like (if photographing from the front) or what the front of the car looks

Figure 6.1: Schematic showing a 3D cube from three unique viewpoints representing different sides of the cube.

like (if photographing from the side). To address this issue, the photographer might choose to photograph the car from a position that captures information about all three dimensions of the car - the width, the height and the length. Such a position might be from the front left of the car at an angle.

In essence, the photographer is performing dimension reduction, by selecting the best possible position to view a 3D object in 2D space. Of course, photography is as much an art as it is a science, and so the decision-making process is about a combination of experience, flair and purpose. In science, we want to be data-driven as much as possible, so that we can make objective, unbiased decisions. Additionally, photography is (almost) always concerned with representing 3D objects in 2D. However, in science, we typically have far more than three dimensions in our data.

To visualise this, imagine we have a cube with each side coloured either red, blue or green (Figure 6.1). As with our hypothetical car, the original dimensions are the width, height and length of the cube (which will be all of equal length here as it is a cube). In our original dimensions, we can either view the width and height (allowing us to view the blue side), width and length (allowing us to see the red side) or the height and length (allowing us to see the green side). However, we can view three sides of the cube in one photo if we choose a better angle from which to view it (Figure 6.2).

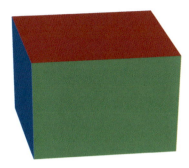

Figure 6.2: Schematic showing a 3D cube from one viewpoint allowing the visualisation of all three dimensions.

6.2 Linear Dimension Reduction: Principal Component Analysis

Numerous techniques exist to carry out dimension reduction, and are best divided into linear and non-linear methods. Let's start with the classic dimension reduction technique called principal component analysis (PCA), a method that is ubiquitous in immunological data analysis in spite of it being a method developed over 100 years ago [26].

In mathematical terminology, PCA is defined as an orthogonal transformation of (potentially) linearly correlated variables into a new co-ordinate system of uncorrelated variables called principal components (often referred to as eigendecomposition of the covariance matrix). Let's put the mathematical aspects of the process to one side, and instead focus on how this definiton relates to our shrewd photographer. In the cube example, our original variables would be the length, width and height of the cube. Our new co-ordinate system would be based on combinations of length, width and height. Figure 6.2 displays the cube using this new co-ordinate system.

Principal component 1 (PC1) is typically shown on the x-axis by convention, with

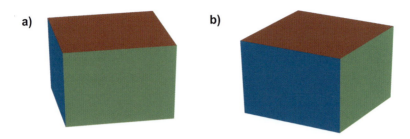

Figure 6.3: Two separate schematics **a)** and **b)** showing the same 3D cube from two different viewpoints, enabling the visualisation of all three dimensions simultaneously. PCA allows the determination of the best viewpoint in a data-driven manner.

PC2 on the y-axis. Figure 6.3 shows how we can represent the cube in 2D from an alternative viewpoint to the original variables (i.e. width, length and height). One of the mathematically beautiful consequences of using PCA is that we can understand how much each of the original variables contribute to each PC, referred to as either the 'weights' or 'loadings'. In Figure 6.3a, we can see that PC1, the x-axis, largely shows the length and height of the cube, and little of its width. Conversely, Figure 6.3b shows mainly the width and height, with little information on the length. Thus, in Figure 6.3a, length and height may have a large weighting, and width would have a smaller weighting. PCA not only allows you to visualise high dimensional data in a 2D figure, but it also allows us the critical ability to *interpret* this reduction in dimensionality. If this seems a little obtuse now, its importance will become clearer later.

Let's look at the code required to conduct a PCA using Python and R.

```
import pandas as pd
import seaborn as sns
import numpy as np

from sklearn.decomposition import PCA
from sklearn.manifold import Isomap, TSNE
from sklearn.discriminant_analysis import LinearDiscriminantAnalysis
from sklearn.preprocessing import scale

import matplotlib.pyplot as plt
sns.set(style='white', font_scale=1.5)
```

```python
np.random.seed(123)

rawData = pd.read_csv('/Users/yourname/Desktop/datascience/data_science_for_
    immunologists.csv')
features = ["alt","viralLoad","sAg"]

myData = rawData[features].dropna().reset_index().drop('index',axis=1)
X = scale(myData[features])
pca = PCA(n_components=2).fit_transform(X)
pca_transformation = pd.DataFrame(pca)
pca_transformation.columns = ['Dimension 1','Dimension 2']
```

```r
install.packages("MASS", dependencies = TRUE)
install.packages("Rtsne", dependencies = TRUE)
install.packages("dimRed", dependencies = TRUE)

library(ggplot2)
library(Rtsne)
library(dimRed)
require(MASS)

set.seed(123)

rawData = read.csv('/Users/yourname/Desktop/datascience/data_science_for_
    immunologists.csv', header=T, na.strings=c("","NA"))
features = c("alt","viralLoad","sAg")

X = scale(na.omit(rawData[,features]), center = TRUE, scale = TRUE)
pca = prcomp(X, scale. = T, center = T)
pca_transformation = as.data.frame(predict(pca, newdata=X))
```

Notice that we need to define beforehand how many components we want to obtain following the dimension reduction. There are two scenarios where we may wish to use dimension reduction - either to be able to plot the data clearly in 2D, or to use it as an input to a clustering or prediction algorithm when we are concerned that we have too many correlated variables in our original dataset. We will discuss the latter scenario in later chapters, so for now let's imagine we want to perform dimension reduction so that we can clearly view our data on a 2D plot. Hence, we

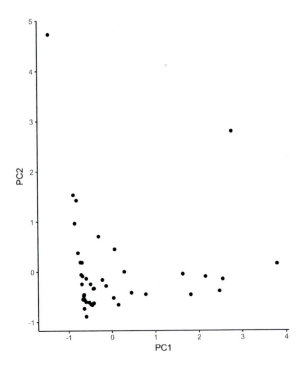

Figure 6.4: A scatterplot depicting principal component 1 (PC1) and principal component 2 (PC2) based on PCA using three features (serum alanine transaminase (ALT); IU/L, HBV viral load (IU/ml) and serum HBsAg titre (IU/ml)).

set n_components=2 when using Python, whereas using R we simply extract the first two principal components after we have performed the PCA.

Once, we've performed PCA, we can plot the data to visualise the 2D projection (Figure 6.4).

```
1  g = sns.lmplot(x='Dimension 1', y='Dimension 2', data=pca_transformation, fit_reg=
       False, size=6)
```

```
1  g = ggplot(pca_transformation, aes(x=PC1, y=PC2)) +
2      geom_point() +
3      theme_classic()
4  g
```

6.3 Non-linear Dimension Reduction

When we are performing PCA, we do so because we want to see the underlying structure in our data as simply as possible. Often, we might want to show that our high dimensional data can be split into groups, and so we hope that PCA preserves these differences even in lower dimensions, so that the variations between groups are still obvious. This might not always be the case though - sometimes our lower dimensional representation may lose the important information from our original data.

In these cases, all is not lost. Many other methods exist to help us in cases where PCA does not perform adequately. These methods fall under the banner of 'non-linear' techniques, so-called because they project the data into lower dimensions using non-linear combinations of the original variables. Going back to our example of photographing a car, this means that if we were to represent the cube in 2D, a small change in position of an item in the original photo may not result in a small change in the position of the item in the lower dimensional, 2D representation (i.e. its change in position in the lower dimensional representation will not be proportional to the change in position in the original photo).

Generally, our approach should be to use a linear method (PCA) first, as it is more easily interpreted. Only if this fails should we consider trying a non-linear method.

6.3.1 Isomap

Compared to PCA, the Isomap is a relatively new technique, first published in 2000 [29]. A motivating example of how Isomap can outperform PCA is shown in Figure 6.5. Suppose we have a dataset where the overriding relationship evident within the data resembles a horseshoe (Figure 6.5a). Figure 6.5b shows how this data would be represented if PCA was used to reduce the dimensionality (i.e. project the 2D horseshoe shape on to a 1D line). Using PCA, the overall structure of the data is lost, in that the points along the horseshoe are no longer located next to each other when represented in 1D via PCA. This is because PCA is solely concerned with the distances between each pair of points.

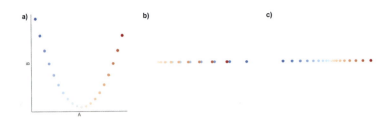

Figure 6.5: **a)** Hypothetical data depicting a non-linear dataset whose shape resembles a horseshoe. PCA has misleadingly placed red and blue points together in the lower dimensional projection in **b)** whereas Isomap has better preserved the structure of the horseshoe-shaped dataset in lower dimensions in **c)**.

However, Isomap takes this concept one step further. To begin, it first determines the nearest X neighbours to every data point, which helps to define local structure (Figure 6.5c). The next step is then to determine the distance between each pair of points by traversing only the nearest neighbours of each point (i.e. this means that in Figure 6.5c, the distance between point 1 and point 6 is actually the distance from point 1 to 2, plus the distance from point 2 to 3, 3 to 4, 4 to 5 and finally 5 to 6). Once this step is complete, PCA-like dimension reduction is performed on these distances (it actually performs multidimensional scaling (MDS) but you can think of MDS as very similar to PCA). The consequence of computing distances between pairs of points in terms of the X nearest neighbours is that the overall structure of the data is more likely to be preserved.

Now let's take a look at how we can do this in Python and R. The visualisation of our data using Isomap is shown in Figure 6.6.

```
myData = rawData[features].dropna().reset_index().drop('index',axis=1)
X = scale(myData[['alt','viralLoad','sAg']])
isomap = Isomap(n_neighbors=5, n_components=2).fit_transform(X)
isomap_transformation = pd.DataFrame(isomap)
isomap_transformation.columns = ['Dimension 1','Dimension 2']
g = sns.lmplot(x='Dimension 1', y='Dimension 2', data=isomap_transformation, fit_
    reg=False, size=6)
```

```
X = scale(na.omit(rawData[,features]), center = TRUE, scale = TRUE)
isomap_transformation <- as.data.frame(embed(X, "Isomap", knn = 10)@apply(X)@data)
```

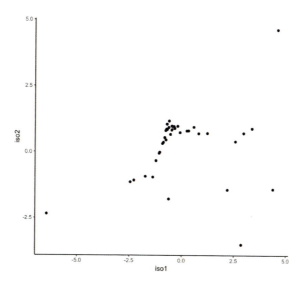

Figure 6.6: A scatterplot depicting dimension reduction using Isomap, based on three original features (serum alanine transaminase (ALT); IU/L, HBV viral load (IU/ml) and serum HBsAg titre (IU/ml)).

```
3   g = ggplot(isomap_transformation, aes(x=iso1, y=iso2)) +
4       geom_point() +
5       theme_classic()
6   g
```

6.3.2 t-SNE

t-SNE (t-distributed stochastic neightbour embedding) is an award-winning method for dimension reduction [30] and is being used for the analysis of flow cytometry data (in the form of the commercial viSNE tool [31] - a full example of using tSNE as part of a pipeline to analyse flow cytometry data is included in Chapter 8). tSNE works on the premise that a 'good' representation in lower dimensions should preserve the distribution of distances between points in the original, high dimensional dataset. This is done by minimising the difference between the distributions of distances in high and lower dimensional space (this is called minimising the Kullback-Leibler divergence of the two distributions).

When the data contains a large number of observations, constructing a distribution of distances over all pairs of points is computationally demanding, so to save time only the X nearest neightbours are considered. This value of X is loosely encoded in the 'perplexity' parameter that the user chooses when running the algorithm. Thus, if the user chooses a larger perplexity, a larger number of nearest neighbours is used. Typically, you should choose a value between 5 and 50, with a larger value chosen for datsets with more observations.

tSNE is undoubtedly a brilliant, extremely useful technique that can learn excellent lower dimensional representations of complex data. However, it is a complex algorithm, and its limitations are not always fully understood by those that use it. You should therefore be aware of the following points when using tSNE as a dimension reduction technique:-

- It may produce different results each time you run the algorithm, even on the same data. This is because minimising the difference between the distance distributions in high and lower dimensional space is a non-convex optimisation problem. This means that the problem cannot be solved exactly, but must be approximated using a technique called gradient descent. Think of this technique as wanting to find the bottom of a volcano - if you parachute into a volcano, you can get to the bottom by taking a series of steps, each step in the direction of the steepest part of the slope. However, if you parachute into a range of volcanoes, it's far more difficult to know which volcano to start walking down, as you don't know which volcano is deepest beforehand. Thus, the different results that tSNE may produce each time it is run are consequences of ending up at the bottom of different volcanoes on each run.

- Distances between groups of points in the lower dimension representation may not mean anything. Of course, the purpose of the algorithm is to faithfully represent the original data. However, the final lower dimension representation, and therefore the distances between groups of points, will depend on how many iterations the algorithm runs for and the chosen value of the perplexity parameter.

- Even random noise may show some structure. The human eye is remarkably good at finding patterns, even when none exist. Likewise, tSNE can sometimes produce plots where clusters of points can be observed in some areas of the plots, but care must be taken when interpreting the data into something meaningful.

- tSNE is computationally demanding compared to most other dimension reduction techniques, and so will take longer to run. It is possible in both R and Python to time how long a piece of code takes to run, and you may want to investigate how you can do this to understand how tSNE compares to other algorithms.

The code to run tSNE is shown below, and the output is shown in Figure 6.7.

```
myData = rawData[features].dropna().reset_index().drop('index',axis=1)
X = scale(myData[features])
tsne = TSNE(n_components=2, perplexity=5, init='pca', learning_rate=100).fit_transform(X)
tsne_transformation = pd.DataFrame(tsne)
tsne_transformation.columns = ['Dimension 1','Dimension 2']
g = sns.lmplot(x='Dimension 1', y='Dimension 2', data=tsne_transformation, fit_reg=False, size=6)
```

```
X = scale(na.omit(rawData[,features]), center = TRUE, scale = TRUE)
tsne = Rtsne(as.matrix(X), perplexity=5, pca=T, eta=100)
tsne_transformation = as.data.frame(tsne$Y)
g = ggplot(tsne_transformation, aes(x=V1, y=V2)) +
  geom_point() +
  theme_classic()
g
```

6.4 Supervised Linear Dimension Reduction: Linear Discriminant Analysis

Linear Discriminant Analysis (LDA) is a generalisation of Fisher's linear discriminant [32] and is similar to PCA in many respects, in that it relies on eigendecomposition to project data into a new coordinate system, and can therefore be thought of as a cousin of PCA. However, the key difference is that LDA is performed in a supervised manner - recall from Chapter 5 that this means we know which class each observation belongs to. In our example that we've been working on throughout this book, this means that we now include the knowledge we have on whether each patient is clinically HBeAg+ or HBeAg- when we are performing the dimension

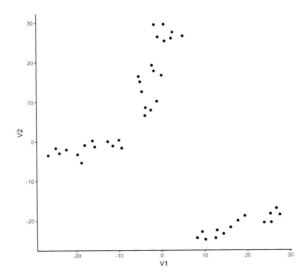

Figure 6.7: A scatterplot depicting dimension reduction using tSNE, based on three original features (serum alanine transaminase (ALT); IU/L, HBV viral load (IU/ml) and serum HBsAg titre (IU/ml)).

reduction.

Briefly, LDA first calculates the mean of each feature from each class. In our example, this means calulcating the mean ALT for HBeAG+ patients, the mean ALT for HBeAG- patients, and then likewise for viral load and HBsAg. Following this, within-class and between-class scatter matrices are calculated and eigendecomposition is then performed on the product of scatter matrices $S_W^{-1} S_B$ (rather than on the covariance matrix as was the case with PCA).

In layman's terms, the scatter matrix S_W here tells us how similar each observation is to the mean of that observation's class. In other words, for all HBeAg+ patients, it tells us how similar each patient is (in terms of ALT, viral load and HBsAg) to the mean ALT, viral load and sAg values across all HBeAg+ patients, and then likewise for HBeAg- patients. The scatter matrix S_B gives us a measure of similarity between classes. In other words, it tells us how similar each class mean is to all observations as a whole. For example, it takes the mean ALT, viral load and sAg for HBeAg+ patients and compares it to all patients in the dataset, and repeats this for HBeAg- patients.

If this is difficult to follow, the key point to remember is that LDA is a supervised dimension reduction method that looks at how different observations are within each class and then between each class. It then translates these differences into a new coordinate system to try and highlight the differences that exist between each class.

Let's take a look at the code.

```
myData = rawData[features].dropna().reset_index().drop('index',axis=1)
X = scale(myData[['alt','viralLoad','sAg']])
y = myData['eAg']

lda = LinearDiscriminantAnalysis(n_components=1).fit(X,y).transform(X)
lda_transformation = pd.DataFrame(lda)
lda_transformation.columns = ['Dimension 1']
lda_transformation['eAg'] = pd.Series(myData['eAg'].values)
```

```
X_unscaled = na.omit(rawData[,c("alt","viralLoad","sAg","eAg")])
X = cbind( X_unscaled[,c("alt","viralLoad","sAg")], X_unscaled$eAg)
colnames(X) = c("alt","viralLoad","sAg","eAg")
lda = lda(eAg ~ ., data=X, prior = c(1/2,1/2))
lda_transformation = as.data.frame(predict(lda, newdata=X)$x)
lda_transformation$eAg = X$eAg
```

Note here how we need to define the vector y, as it's a supervised method. Now we can run LDA on this data.

Finally, we can plot the results. The result here will be a little different to what we have seen above. In all the previous methods we have used, we've been able to get a 2D projection of our data - reducing the original datset from three features to two. With LDA, we are only able to reduce the data set to $n-1$ dimensions at most, where n is the number of classes in our data (i.e. the number of distinct values in y above). In other words, we are reducing the dimensions in our dataset in the hope that we are able to separate HBeAg+ patients from HBeAg- patients after we have reduced the dimensionality. As there are only $n = 2$ classes here (i.e. HBeAg+ and HBeAg-), LDA will only output $n - 1 = 1$ dimension. This can be viewed in Figure 6.8, produced using the following code.

```
fig, ax = plt.subplots()
sns.stripplot(x="Dimension 1", y='eAg', hue='eAg', data=lda_transformation, jitter
```

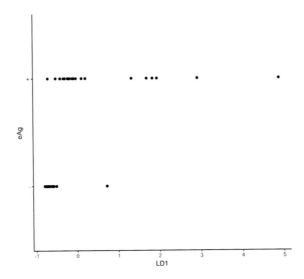

Figure 6.8: Supervised LDA based on three original features (serum alanine transaminase (ALT); IU/L, HBV viral load (IU/ml) and serum HBsAg titre (IU/ml)). LDA differs to other dimension reduction techniques in that it is a supervised technique, and so requires disease categories (labels) for each sample.

```
         = False, split = True, ax = ax)
3    ax.legend_.remove()
4    sns.despine(bottom = False, left=True)
```

```
1    g = ggplot(lda_transformation, aes(x=LD1,y=eAg)) +
2      geom_point() +
3      theme_classic()
4    g
```

From this plot, we can see that we've done a fairly good job of finding just one dimension that linearly separates HBeAg+ patients from HBeAg- patients. Larger values of our new dimension (called Dimension 1 in Figure 6.8) imply a greater chance of the patient being HBeAg-. This leads us nicely to our next Chapter, where we'll look at building predictive models.

Chapter 7

Predicting

When making a prediction, we are typically interested in understanding what will happen in the future based on values we have observed in the present or past. The values that we wish to predict in the future are typically either continuous or binary. Whether we are predicting a continuous or binary outcome will affect what type of predictive model we choose to use.

Continuous outcomes are those that can take any value, both positive and negative as well as zero. As an example, we may wish to predict a patient's serum ALT levels using other clinical attributes such as necroinflammatory score and patient age. As ALT level in a patient is a continuous variable, we would need to use an appropriate method that allows us to make such a prediction.

Conversely, we may want to predict whether a sample is from an HBeAg+ or HBeAg- patient based on HBV viral load and serum HBsAg titre. Here, the presence of the viral antigen, HBeAg, is the outcome we are trying to predict, and is either positive or negative, so we would require a method that can predict a binary variable. We could even take this one step further and try to predict a ternary outcome, such as whether a sample is from a healthy individual (HBeAg-HBsAg- HBV viral load negative), an HBeAg+ or HBeAg- individual with chronic HBV infection. This is called a multi-class classification problem, where we are trying to predict which one of a number (more than 2) of classes a certain observation belongs to.

7.1 Assessing Model Accuracy

It's all very well building a model to predict an outcome, but we should not place blind faith in a model without knowledge of how well we can expect it to perform on new, unseen observations. We would of course have more confidence in a model that could predict an outcome with 95% accuracy compared to one that is only 75% accurate. We also might come to the conclusion that the model with 75% accuracy could be improved, and thus we might be prompted to search for a better model. In such circumstances, we are using model accuracy as a means for selecting the best predictive model.

The metric we use to assess model accuracy depends on what type of outcome we are predicting. Typically, the accuracy of a continuous outcome is judged using mean average percentage error (MAPE), root mean square error (RMSE) or R^2 (recall that this metric was introduced in Chapter 4). Classification problems are often judged by accuracy (i.e. the proportion of correct predictions), F1 score or area under curve (AUC).

Let's look at each of these in turn.

7.1.1 Continuous Outcome: Root Mean Square Error (RMSE)

Root mean square error (RMSE) is defined as: -

$$RMSE = \sqrt{\frac{\sum_{t=1}^{n}(\hat{y}_t - y_t)^2}{n}} \qquad (7.1)$$

It is a simple measure of the sum of differences between predicted outcome ($\hat{y}$) and actual outcome (y) over a set of n observations (such as n patients).

7.1.2 Continuous Outcome: Mean Accuracy Percentage Error (MAPE)

Mean accuracy percentage error (MAPE) is defined as: -

$$MAPE = \frac{100}{n}\sum_{t=1}^{n}|\frac{y_t - \hat{y}_t}{y_t}| \qquad (7.2)$$

It is a better measure than RMSE as it represents the error as a proportion of the value of the target variable. In other words, the value of MAPE is independent of the scale of the target variable.

7.1.3 Continuous Outcome: R^2

The R^2 metric tells us how much of the variance of the continuous target variable is captured by the predictive model: -

$$\bar{R}^2 = 1 - \frac{SS_{res}}{SS_{tot}} \qquad (7.3)$$

where

$SS_{res} = \sum_i (y_i - f_i)^2$ is the residual sum of squares, and $SS_{tot} = \sum_i (y_i - \bar{y})^2$ is the total sum of squares.

Thus, R^2 will be equal to one when the residual sum of squares and the total sum of squares are equal, implying that the model has fit the data very well. The residual sum of squares tells us how well the model fits the target variable of interest, with a better model giving a small residual sum of squares. The total sum of squares tells us how 'easy' it should be to fit a model to the target variable (a target variable that is always very close to a particular value is intuitively easier to predict than one which varies widely) - a larger total sum of squares means that the variable is harder to predict.

R^2, sometimes called the coefficient of determination, will be nearly equal to zero when a predictive model fits the data badly. In theory, the value of R^2 can be less than zero, when the residuals are greater than the total sum of squares. In such circumstances, this is telling us that the model is even worse than one which simply predicts the mean of the target variable.

7.1.4 Categorical Outcome: Accuracy, False Positive Rate and False Negative Rate

The accuracy of a classification model is the proportion of observations that are successfully classified: -

$$A = \frac{TP + TN}{TP + FP + TN + FN} \tag{7.4}$$

where TP, TN, FP and FN are respectively the number of true positives (TP), true negatives (TN), false positives (FP) and false negatives (FN). We want to identify as many of the true positives and true negatives as possible, while limiting the number of false positives and false negatives from our model.

Sometimes, it is necessary to report more about the nature of the predictions our model makes. In other words, as well as reporting simply how accurate it is, we might also wish to report the false positive rate (FPR) and false negative rate (FNR).

The FPR is defined as

$$FPR = \frac{FP}{FP + TN}, \tag{7.5}$$

and the FNR as

$$FNR = \frac{FN}{TP + FN}. \tag{7.6}$$

These metrics help us to identify where our model is performing badly. For example, imagine a dataset which contains ninety healthy controls and just ten observations from patients with disease. We could create a 'predictive model' that just predicts *healthy control* regardless of whatever data we have on each sample, and obtain an 'accuracy' of 90%. In some clinical settings, such high predictive accuracy may be deemed very good. However, if we were to look more closely, we would see that while the false positive rate of 0% is very good, the false negative rate of 100% is terrible. The context of the model will determine whether you would consider a false positive or false negative more harmful, and may play some role in guiding which model you ultimately choose.

7.1.5 Categorical Outcome: Area Under Curve (AUC)

The receiver operating characteristic (ROC) curve is a graphical means of displaying how well a classification model performs. The false positive rate (FPR) is shown on

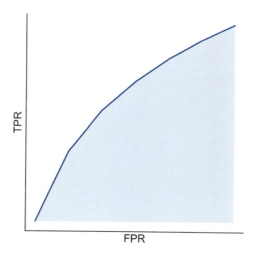

Figure 7.1: Graphical representation of a receiver operator characteristic (ROC) curve, which can be used to demonstrate model accuracy. The shaded area represents area under curve (AUC). Accurate models are found in the top left quadrant, with high true positive rates and low false positive rates.

the x-axis, with the true positive rate (TPR) shown on the y-axis. The graph shows how the FPR and TPR vary as the classification boundary of the model varies. We will discuss this in more detail later, but for the time being consider a simple example in the context of HBV. Patients can be clinically classified as 'low-level carriers' with inactive disease, or 'immune actives' with high-level viral replication. If we were to categorise a patient solely on HBV viral load, then our classification boundary might be 2000 IU/ml. The ROC curve shows how well the model will perform as that threshold is varied.

We would ideally like our model to have a large TPR and small FPR. Models with these properties are found in the top left corner of Figure 7.1. We can summarise how well a model performs by using what is known as the area under curve (AUC). The larger the AUC, the better the model, as it means that we are are likely to be able to choose a threshold (e.g. for viral load in classifying disease category) that gives a model with a large TPR and small FPR.

7.1.6 F1 Score

An additional measure that can be used to summarise the relationship between TP, FN and FP is the F1 score. Specifically, the F1 score is the harmonic mean of precision and recall.

The recall of a model tells us of all the actual positives, what proportion are predicted to be positive. For example, for a model that is designed to detect the presence of HBeAg in patients, recall tells us the proportion of HBeAg+ patients that our model detects.

$$r = \frac{TP}{TP + FN} \tag{7.7}$$

The precision of a model tells us of all the predicted positives, what proportion are actual positives. For example, precision tells us of all the predicted HBeAg+ patients, what proportion are actually HBeAg+.

$$p = \frac{TP}{TP + FP} \tag{7.8}$$

F1 score is then defined as

$$F1 = \frac{2pr}{p + r} \tag{7.9}$$

F1 score is an important metric in situations where our cohort of samples is unbalanced and contains far more HBeAg+ patients, choosing a model with a good F1 score stops us from taking the 'easy option' of predicting that every patient is HBeAg.

7.2 Frameworks to Calculate Accuracy Metrics

The importance of a rigorous framework for assessing model accuracy cannot be underestimated. Suppose we have collected data from 50 individuals, and want to build a predictive model to tell us whether a patient has a certain disease or not. At first glance you may think it would suffice to fit a model to those 50 patients and consequently report how well the model fits the data - we would then choose whichever model fits best.

On second glance, it should become apparent that this is not the best way to go about the task. Imagine that we are comparing two models. Model A is a very simple model with only one parameter that can change its value depending on what the data looks like, and model B is very complex with a hundred parameters that can change their value based on the data. It is very likely that model B will fit the data better as it is a more complex model, but if we use this alone then we will not necessarily choose the model that best generalises to other patients. Thus, we need a better approach to selecting a model and assessing how accurate it is.

The above framework can be improved by separating individuals randomly into different groups. The key idea is that we want to use some samples to fit the model, and a different set of samples to assess how accurate that model is. In the world of data science and machine learning, these two phases of fitting a model and assessing its accuracy are called *training* and *testing* respectively. We first train a model using some samples and then test the model using different samples. Following training and testing, a final *validation* phase can be used if two or more models are being compared over the training and testing phases.

In an ideal world, we would have a dataset consisting of hundreds, or even thousands, of observations. However, this is often not feasible in many real world settings; if the observations are events in a flow cytometry sample then it would seem reasonable to assume that we will have thousands of observations. But if the observations are patients in a clinical study, then it is much more likely that we will have far fewer observations, potentially no more than thirty or forty. Whilst a training-testing-validating framework is always advised, the exact manner in which this is done should be based on how many observations are available to you.

The most intuitive framework to train and test a model is the straightforward hold-out method. Here, we would partition our observations into two randomly chosen groups, g_1 and g_2 say. We would then simply use g_1 to train the model and g_2 to test the model. g_1 and g_2 will not neccesarily be the same size; typically g_1 will contain more observations (up to 70%) to ensure that the model is trained as accurately as possible.

An extension of this framework used to train and test a model is called k-fold cross validation. The idea is that you iteratively partition your data into randomly chosen train and test groups of equal size (i.e. the same number of observations in each group) and determine accuracy on the test set on each iteration. The value of k determines into how many groups the data is split on each iteration. For example, 3-fold cross validation involves splitting the data into 3 randomly chosen groups of observations, groups A, B and C, say. These groups are typically referred to as folds, giving the framework its name. The approach involves first training a model on group A and B, and testing the model on C, then training on A and C and testing on B, then finally training on B and C and testing on A.

Hopefully from this explanation it becomes apparent that each observation will always be used for testing once, and only once. However, this need not be the case, and an alternative framework exists called bootstrapping. As with k-fold cross-validation, this technique involves an iterative approach, but instead of using fixed partitions containing equal numbers of observations in each group, bootstrapping randomly samples observations from the whole data set with replacement. This means that on each iteration, the training and test groups will (likely) contain different observations and be of different sizes each time. The benefit of this technique is that it allows you to easily calculate confidence intervals for your estimate of model accuracy, so that we understand not only how well we would expect the model to perform on new data, but also how much we would expect that performance to vary from sample to sample.

Now we have a rigorous framework to assess model accuracy, we can look at how to predict a continuous outcome.

7.3 Predicting Continuous Outcomes

7.3.1 Linear Regression

The most well-known prediction technique is one that we've already covered in an earlier Chapter; linear regression [26]. Recall that linear regression gives us the following capabilities: -

1. The 'slope' of the straight line that best fits the relationship between your

chosen target variable and the predictors.

2. The 'intercept' of the straight line that best fits the relationship between your two chosen variables, which tells us what the value of the target variable is when all other predictors are equal to zero.

3. A quantification of how well the target variable is predicted by the predictor variables. This is the so-called R^2 value, which is near 0 when the line is not a good fit and near 1 when the model provides a good fit.

4. A predictive model which gives us the most likely value of the target variable for a given set of values of our predictor variables.

In our original example in Chapter 4, we only used one variable, the frequency of gMDSC, to predict total white blood cell count in our patients with chronic HBV infection. We can of course use more than one variable to predict our target, so let's now turn our attention to predicting ALT by including more than one predictor.

We will first need to import the relevant packages and libraries for the code in this Chapter.

```
1  import numpy as np
2  import pandas as pd
3
4  from sklearn.linear_model import LogisticRegression, LinearRegression
5  from sklearn.ensemble import RandomForestRegressor
6  from sklearn.svm import LinearSVC
7  from sklearn.model_selection import LeaveOneOut
8  from sklearn.feature_selection import SelectKBest, mutual_info_classif, f_classif, RFE
9  from sklearn.preprocessing import scale
10 from sklearn.metrics import f1_score
11
12 rawData = pd.read_csv('/Users/yourname/Desktop/datascience/data_science_for_immunologists.csv')
13
14 target = 'alt'
15 features = ['gMDSC','age','viralLoad','sAg']
16
17 myData = rawData[features+[target]].dropna().reset_index().drop('index',axis=1)
18 myData[features] = scale(myData[features])
```

```
1  install.packages("caret", dependencies=TRUE)
2  install.packages("glmnet", dependencies=TRUE)
3  install.packages("MLmetrics", dependencies = TRUE)
4  install.packages("mpmi", dependencies = TRUE)
5
6  library(caret)
7  library(glmnet)
8  library(MLmetrics)
9  library(mpmi)
10
11 rawData = read.csv('/Users/yourname/Desktop/datascience/data_science_for_
       immunologists.csv', header=T, na.strings=c("","NA"))
12
13 target = 'alt'
14 features = c('gMDSC','age','viralLoad','sAg')
15
16 myData = na.omit(rawData[,c(features,target)])
17 myData[,features] = scale(myData[,features])
```

Not that we have got all the functions and packages that we need, we can begin training and testing our model using leave-one-out cross-validation.

```
1  loo = LeaveOneOut()
2  results = pd.DataFrame({'Prediction':[], 'Actual':[], 'PercentError':[]})
3
4  for train_index, test_index in loo.split(myData):
5      X_train, X_test = myData[features].iloc[train_index], myData[features].iloc[
           test_index]
6      y_train, y_test = myData[target].iloc[train_index], myData[target].iloc[test_
           index]
7
8      model = LinearRegression()
9      model.fit(X_train, y_train)
10
11     prediction = model.predict(X_test)[0]
12
13     results = results.append({'Prediction':prediction, 'Actual':y_test.values[0],
           'PercentError':100*np.abs(y_test.values[0] - prediction)/y_test.values[0]},
           ignore_index=True)
14
15 model.coef_
16
```

```r
17  print("MAPE = ",results.PercentError.sum() / results.shape[0],"%")
```

```r
1   numObs = dim(myData)[1]
2   predictions = c()
3   actuals = myData$alt
4
5   for (i in c(1:numObs)){
6
7     train = myData[-i,]
8     test = myData[i,]
9
10    linear_regression = lm(alt ~ ., data=train)
11
12    predictions = c(predictions, predict(linear_regression, test))
13
14  }
15
16  results = data.frame( actuals, predictions)
17  results$percenterror = 100 * abs(results$actuals - results$prediction) / results$actuals
18  results
19
20  print(paste("MAPE = ", sum(results$percenterror) / dim(results)[1],"%"))
```

We have used MAPE to determine how well our model performs on the test data - recall that this tells us how well we can expect the model to perform on unseen samples that we have never encountered before. Our MAPE value of 95.4% tells us that our predictive model is not very effective, so let's try another predictive method to see if we can improve this.

7.3.2 Random Forests

Random forests [33] are a type of ensemble learning method that can be used for both regression and classification tasks, but we will focus on using them for regression tasks here in order to predict a continuous outcome. Ensemble learning methods are so-called because they combine the outputs of many indiviudal algorithms to produce a better performing predictive model. In the case of random

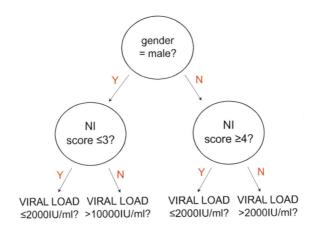

Figure 7.2: Schematic depicting a hypothetical decision tree to be used as an intuitive method for making predictions of continuous and discrete target variables, based on the notion of following a path through the tree using feature values of the observation you are trying to predict.

forests, they combine the output of many decision trees, where each individual decision tree predicts a value for the target continuous variable.

Decision trees can be thought of as a collection of 'branches', 'nodes' and 'leaves'. Branches represent decisions taken on the values of input variables, whereas leaves give the predicted value of the target variable based on decisions made at previous nodes higher up the tree. Figure 7.2 shows schematically a hypothetical decision tree using two input variables, necroinflammatory score and gender, where we are attempting to predict the HBV viral load in our chronically infected cohort.

How do we decide which order to ask the questions in a decision tree? These decisions are made based on which feature reduces the standard deviation of the target variable the most if it is used to split the node. For example, in the above example, if patients with a necroinflammatory score of 1 always have a viral load of 400 IU/ml and with a necroinflammatory score of 5 always have a viral load of 50000 IU/ml, then this is an ideal candidate to base a split on, as in doing so we reduce the standard deviation from a group of patients with viral loads ranging from 400 - 50000 IU/ml to two distinct sets of patients each with zero standard deviation in viral load.

Decision trees are the building blocks on which random forests are built. Decision trees have a tendency to 'overfit' the training data, in that they are flexible enough to fit the training data very well, but fail to generalise accurately to new observations (i.e. the test set).

Random forests overcome this issue by subsampling features and observations at random (hence the name), so that each tree in the forest has only a subset of all features and observations. The output from each individual tree is then aggregated and averaged to produce the final output from the random forest (i.e. the prediction of HBV viral load would be the average predicted HBV viral load across all decision trees).

Given the above description, you are hopefully now asking yourself how many trees each forest has (*n*), and how deep each forest is (*depth*). These are hyperparameters of the algorithm that the data scientist must define. The values of these hyperparameters can drastically affect the output and therefore the accuracy of the model. As such these hyperparameters should be chosen such that they produce the best output when training the model. Selecting hyperparameter values is not something we will cover in this Chapter, but is a very important aspect of building a strong predictive model. The concept of selecting the best hyperparameter values is covered in Chapter 8.

Now that we have all the background to understand what is happening, let's take a look at random forests in action.

```
1  loo = LeaveOneOut()
2  results = pd.DataFrame({'Prediction':[], 'Actual':[], 'PercentError':[]})
3
4  for train_index, test_index in loo.split(myData):
5      X_train, X_test = myData[features].iloc[train_index], myData[features].iloc[test_index]
6      y_train, y_test = myData[target].iloc[train_index], myData[target].iloc[test_index]
7
8      model = RandomForestRegressor(n_estimators=10, random_state=123)
9      model.fit(X_train, y_train)
10
11     prediction = model.predict(X_test)[0]
12
13     results = results.append({'Prediction':prediction, 'Actual':y_test.values[0],
```

```
       'PercentError':100*np.abs(y_test.values[0] - prediction)/y_test.values[0]},
       ignore_index=True)

print("MAPE = ",results.PercentError.sum() / results.shape[0],"%")
```

```
numObs = dim(myData)[1]
predictions = c()
actuals = myData$alt
set.seed(123)

for (i in c(1:numObs)){

  train = myData[-i,]
  test = myData[i,]

  rf = randomForest::randomForest( alt ~ ., data=train, ntree=10)

  predictions = c(predictions, predict(rf, test))

}

results = data.frame( actuals, predictions)
results$percenterror = 100 * abs(results$actuals - results$prediction) / results$actuals
results

print(paste("MAPE = ", sum(results$percenterror) / dim(results)[1],"%"))
```

Once again assessing model accuracy, you should obtain a MAPE of 87% using the Python code and 73.2% using the R code. While we have improved the MAPE compared to using linear regression, a MAPE this large indicates further work would be needed if we wanted to publish the results or use the model for further predictions.

7.4 Predicting Binary Outcomes

So far we have dealt with predicting continuous outcomes, but we will often also want to predict categorical outcomes. In most scenarios, we will want to predict an outcome that can take one of two values - so-called binary classification problems. Sometimes we may have more than two groups to which an observation may belong, and in such circumstances we can extend binary classification frameworks to cope with such multi-class data sets. However, to start with, let's just consider binary classification problems.

Suppose we wanted to build a classification model that predicts whether a patient has active or inactive disease based solely on viral load. Suppose that we also have HBV viral load measurements from two 'low-level carriers' with inactive disease and from two 'immune actives' with active, ongoing disease. If the HBV viral loads in the low-level carriers are 400 IU/ml and 1000 IU/ml, and HBV viral loads in the immune actives are 50000 IU/ml and 120000 IU/ml then we would qualitatively conclude that a higher HBV viral load is indicative of active disease. But, based on these data points, what threshold should be chosen as a cut-off for determining active and inactive disease?

Intuitively, this cut-off should lie somewhere between the highest measured HBV viral load in low-level carriers and the lowest observed HBV viral load in immune active patients. We may want to base our cut-off on observations from all patients, but a simple, and arguably better, approach is to use just the most extreme value in each group. In our example above, the most extreme values in each group are 1000 IU/ml in low-level carriers and 50000 IU/ml in immune actives. Based on these two observations, the best cut-off to choose would be the midpoint between the two values; 24500 IU/ml.

7.4.1 Support Vector Machine

The above example, though somewhat arbitrary, illustrates the key idea behind a classic binary classification model; the support vector machine (SVM) [34]. SVM work by finding the best threshold on which to split obervations into two groups. Recall that in Chapter 5 we introduced the concept of **unsupervised** learning, where we have no underlying labels on which to base the clustering. SVM are **supervised** methods, which rely on labelled observations to train the model so that it can be used in the future to classify new observations.

Of course, when we only have one feature on which to build a predictive model,

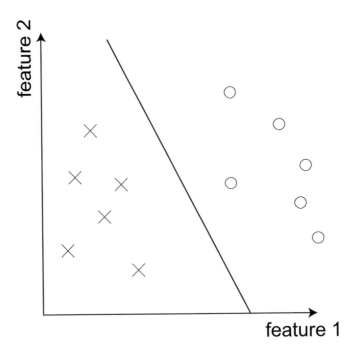

Figure 7.3: Graphical representation of a hypothetical dataset with two features (features 1 and 2) separated by a decision boundary established by using a support vector machine that splits observations according to their class label.

it may seem slightly trivial to select a cutoff value as above. But things get more complicated when we have many features on which to build a predictive model. In these cases, SVM come into their own as accurate, robust and scalable models, but the principal idea remains the same. The only difference is that the threshold used to distinguish the two groups becomes more complex. When one feature is used to build the predictive model, the threshold takes the form of a single value. When two features are used to build a predictive model, the threshold becomes what is commonly called a decision boundary, as it is defined by a combination of two features. Figure 7.3 shows this concept.

The decision boundary when basing the predictive model on two features takes the form of a straight line, and when using three features it takes the form of a 2-D plane. In general, when using n features to build a predictive model, the decision boundary will be a $n-1$-D hyperplane; a hyperplane can be thought of as a straight line that generalises to many more dimensions.

The SVM operates by minimising the distance between the decision boundary and

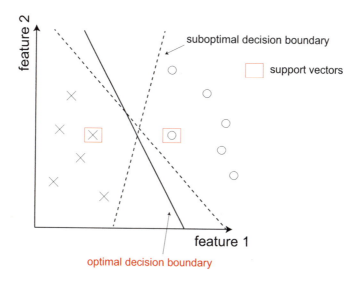

Figure 7.4: Graphical representation of a hypothetical dataset with two features (features 1 and 2) separated by multiple decision boundaries established using a support vector machine that splits observations according to their class label. Suboptimal decision boundaries (dashed lines) do not maximise the distance between the nearest observations from each class. The optimal choice (solid line) is the one which provides the biggest distance from the nearest observations of each class. Support vectors (highlighted in red) are those observations that lie nearest the decision boundary.

the nearest observations from each group (Figure 7.4). These 'nearest observations' are referred to as support vectors, giving the method its name. New observations are classified by comparison to these support vectors, making the method scalable to datasets with a large number of features (for example, gene expression profiles based on thousands of genes; see Chapter 8 for a full, working study using SVM to build a predictive model from gene expression data).

Hopefully Figures 7.3 and 7.4 spark a further question in your data science brain - what happens when we cannot separate the two classes with a straight line (or hyperplane more generally), i.e. what happens when the data is not linearly separable? Luckily, SVM are still more than able to cope with such circumstances. In these cases the decision boundary is moved to account for observations that would fall on the wrong side of the decision boundary, and the amount by which it moves is determined by a hyperparameter called C. Larger values of C penalise outliers more heavily. The correct value to choose for C will vary from dataset to dataset, and can usually be selected via a grid search. This simply involves checking how well each value of C performs during model testing and selecting the best performer. We will look at how to do this in an example shortly.

The other trick that the SVM has up its sleeve is its ability to implicitly fit a non-linear decision boundary. In other words, the separating hyperplane need not be linear, and the straight lines in Figure 7.4 can actually be a lines of arbitrary shape through a clever trick. This clever trick can be thought of as transforming the data in such a way that after the transformation the data becomes linearly separable. It is a remarkable modification, and one that is not always easily understood. Let's consider a hypothetical example in Figure 7.5a. Here, we have two hypothetical features called A and B shown respectively on the x- and y-axis. It should be clear that no straight line can be found to separate the red and blue points. However, if we map each point such that a new feature called Z is defined as:

$$Z = A^2 + B^2, \qquad (7.10)$$

then we suddenly find that we can indeed split the red and blue points with a straight line. It's easiest to see this by means of a simple plot, showing A and $Z = A^2 + B^2$ on the x- and y-axis respectively (Figure 7.5b). This clever trick is referred to as the kernel trick, and is a commonly used phenomenon in many branches of machine learning.

Once we have trained our model and found the best choice of hyperplane to separate our training data, we can predict the class of new observations by calculating which side of the hyperplane they lie.

$$Class(x) = sign(xw_\prime + w_0) \qquad (7.11)$$

In other words, when using a linear kernel, it's simply a case of multiplying the value of each feature by its corresponding weight w_i, adding a constant $_0$, and determining whether this is positive or negative. This amounts to determining which side of the hyperplane it lies. It's very important to note though that this is not the case when using the kernel trick above - when deciding whether to use the kernel trick, you are usually faced with a trade-off between a model that's easy

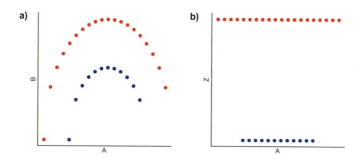

Figure 7.5: Hypothetical illustration of the kernel trick. When a linear decision boundary cannot discriminate between classes in the original dataset in **a)**, i.e. there is no possible way to find a linear hyperplane that will split the red and blue points, the kernel trick can be used to transform the original features (A and B) into a new feature space (i.e. using the function $Z = A^2 + B^2$), where we are able to find a linear hyperplane that splits the red and blue points in **b)**.

to interpret but may not be as accurate in all situations (linear kernel) versus a model that is (potentially) more accurate, but is far harder to interpret (non-linear kernel trick).

Now we have the basic understanding of what SVM does and how it works, let's look at a real example using a linear kernel.

```
target = 'eAg'
features = ['gMDSC','age','alt','viralLoad','sAg','niScore']

myData = rawData[features+[target]].dropna().reset_index().drop('index',axis=1)
myData[features] = scale(myData[features])

loo = LeaveOneOut()
results = pd.DataFrame({'Prediction':[],'Actual':[]})

for train_index, test_index in loo.split(myData):
    X_train, X_test = myData[features].iloc[train_index], myData[features].iloc[test_index]
    y_train, y_test = myData[target].iloc[train_index], myData[target].iloc[test_index]

    model = LinearSVC()
    model.fit(X_train, y_train)

```

```python
        prediction = model.predict(X_test)[0]

        results = results.append({'Prediction':prediction, 'Actual':y_test.values[0]},
            ignore_index=True)

    print("Model Accuracy = ",results[results.Actual==results.Prediction].shape[0] /
        results.shape[0])
```

```r
target = 'eAg'
features = c('gMDSC','age','alt','viralLoad','sAg','niScore')

myData = na.omit(rawData[,c(features,target)])
myData[,features] = scale(myData[,features])
myData$eAg = as.factor(myData$eAg)

numObs = dim(myData)[1]
predictions = c()
actuals = myData$eAg
set.seed(123)

for (i in c(1:numObs)){

    train = myData[-i,]
    test = myData[i,]

    svm = train( eAg ~ ., data=train, method="svmLinear", preProcess=c("center","scale"))

    predictions = c(predictions, toString(predict(svm, newdata=test)))

}

results = data.frame( actuals, predictions)
results$correct = (results$actuals == results$predictions)
print(paste("Accuracy = ",100 * dim(results[results$correct==TRUE,])[1] / dim(results)[1], "%"))
```

In the case of linear kernels only, the size of the weight tells us how important the feature is in making the prediction. Hopefully this seems quite intuitive - if we're only interested in whether Equation 7.11 is positive or negative, then features with larger weights will have more of a say in whether the sign is positive or negative. The fact that new observations are classified by using the weights associated with each feature makes the SVM a good predictive model to use when performing something known as feature selection. We will introduce this topic later in the Chapter before using SVMs in Chapter 8 to identify gene signatures in cancer patients.

7.4.2 Logistic Regression

Perhaps the most frequently used predictive model of binary outcomes, logistic regression [35] has the added bonus of calculating the probability of a given binary outcome as part of its natural framework. Whilst it is also possible to calculate the probability of a binary outcome using SVM, the way in which logistic regression works means that the probability is calculated automatically, rather than as an additional step as with the SVM.

The logistic function provides the framework that relates features to the binary outcome of interest. Suppose, for example, that we wish to predict whether a patient is HBeAG+ or HBeAg- based on viral load. We might hypothesise that a higher HBV viral load (VL) means a patient is more likely to be HBeAg+. Using logistic regression, we can estimate the probability that a patient is HBeAg+ given their viral load using the logistic function:

$$P(eAg+|VL) = \frac{1}{1+e^{-(\beta_0+\beta_1 VL)}}. \tag{7.12}$$

β_0 and β_1 are coefficients to be determined when training the predictive model, and is usually done by a technique called gradient descent. The way in which these coefficients are determined is not of significance here, but it is important to note what this logistic function means in practice. If β_1 is found to be greater than 0 by gradient descent, then larger values of HBV viral loads are predicted to be indicative of a greater chance of a patient being HBeAg+. This is because the expression $\exp-(\beta_0+\beta_1 VL)$ will decrease in value as viral load increases, and so the expression $\frac{1}{1+\exp-(\beta_0+\beta_1 VL)}$ will increase in value.

The logistic function is non-linear, taking the shape of an 'S' shaped curve. The exact shape is determined by the values of β_0 and β_1, which in turn are determined

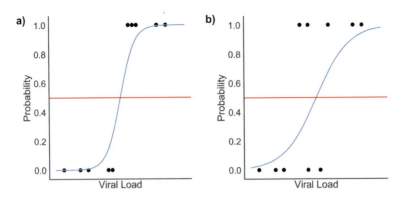

Figure 7.6: Graphical representation of two hypothetical datasets, where logistic regression has been used to build a predictive model that fits an 'S'-shaped curve to relate HBV viral load to the probability of a patient being HBeAG+. In **a)**, the 'S'-shaped curve is sharper compared to **b)**, reflecting the fact that patients who are HBeAg+ in the dataset in **a)** can be more easily separated based on HBV viral loads compared to those in **b)**.

by the nature of the training data. As is often the case, a better understanding usually comes from visualising what is happening (Figure 7.6).

In Figure 7.6, the y-axis represents the presence or absence of HBeAg in each of our patients, so only takes one of two values (0 or 1). The x-axis represents their HBV viral load. Thus, if we see many data points in the bottom left corner of Figure 7.6 and many data points in the top right corner, we would be able to develop a very accurate predictive model. In Figure 7.6a, the shape of the S-curve (the logistic function) is very sharp, as this best fits the data points shown in that case.

However, things are not always so easy, and often we end up with points in all four corners of the grid with many real world data sets. In such cases, the shape of the curve will be far broader, in an attempt to better fit the data and reflect the fact that we have less confidence in predicting which class a given observation will fall into (Figure 7.6b). Why is the logistic function so useful in the context of binary classification? This is largely due to the fact that the function outputs values that always fall between zero and one - giving a natural way to convert a given value of viral load into a probability of whether someone is likely to be HBeAg+ or HBeAg-.

Let's now see how we can use logistic regression in R and Python.

```python
1  loo = LeaveOneOut()
2  results = pd.DataFrame({'Prediction':[], 'Actual':[]})
3
4  for train_index, test_index in loo.split(myData):
5      X_train, X_test = myData[features].iloc[train_index], myData[features].iloc[test_index]
6      y_train, y_test = myData[target].iloc[train_index], myData[target].iloc[test_index]
7
8      model = LogisticRegression(random_state=123)
9      model.fit(X_train, y_train)
10
11     prediction = model.predict(X_test)[0]
12
13     results = results.append({'Prediction':prediction, 'Actual':y_test.values[0]}, ignore_index=True)
14
15
16 print("Model Accuracy = ",results[results.Actual==results.Prediction].shape[0] / results.shape[0])
```

```
1  numObs = dim(myData)[1]
2  predictions = c()
3  actuals = myData$eAg
4  set.seed(123)
5
6  for (i in c(1:numObs)){
7
8    train = myData[-i,]
9    test = myData[i,]
10
11   log_reg = glmnet( as.matrix(train[,features]), as.factor(train[,target]), alpha=0, family="binomial")
12
13   predictions = c(predictions, predict(log_reg, as.matrix(test[,features]), s=0.01, type='class'))
14
15 }
16
17 results = data.frame( actuals, predictions)
18 results$correct = (results$actuals == results$predictions)
19 print(paste("Accuracy = ",100 * dim(results[results$correct==TRUE,])[1] / dim(
```

```
results)[1], "%"))
```

Thus, we have managed to built an accurate model using logistic regression, with accuracy of 83%. However, as mentioned before, accuracy can sometimes be a flawed metric, and we may want to instead use a metric that takes into acount the relationship between TP, FP, TN and FN. To do this, we can use the F1 score described earlier in the Chapter.

```
f1_score( results['Actual'], results['Prediction'])
```

```
F1_Score( results$actuals, results$predictions)
```

An F1 score of 0.81 assures us we have built a model we can rely on to detect whether the sample came from a HBeAg positive or negative individual.

7.5 Predictions with Text

Up to this point, we have made predictions using only numerical features. In some situations, we may want to make predictions using text. For example, we may wish to build a predictive model of diesase based on text descriptions of clinical symptoms of patients, or we may want to build a model that uses T cell receptor (TCR) sequences to predict disease outcome.

Ultimately, building such models relies on the same approach discussed above - we will want to use cross validation within a train and test framework to determine how our model performs. Likewise, we will want to use the techniques introduced earlier in the Chapter, such as SVM, to make our predictions. SVM can only take numerical data as input, so the question is how can we represent text data numerically, in a way that preserves the information contained in the text.

One of the most popular approaches to represent text data numerically is to use the bag-of-words approach. Recall that the features we used to predict the presence or absence of HBeAg in our patients were gMDSC, age, ALT, HBV viral load, HBsAg and necroinflammatory score - the values of these six features determined whether a patient was predicted to be HBeAg+ or HBeAg-. Using a bag-of-words approach, the words themselves become the features, and the frequencies of each word in a 'document' form the basis of the prediction.

It should be noted at this point the terminology that is used by convention here - many *words* make up a *document*, and many documents make up a *corpus*. In the case of immunological data, we may consider our words to be TCR sequences or even single amino acids, our document to be a *.fastq* file and our corpus to be the set of all *.fastq* files from several patients (some of whom may be healthy and some may have disease). In this scenario, we would want to predict which files (i.e. *documents*) are from patients with a particular disease and which are from healthy controls, based on features of TCR sequences contained within the files. Thus, it is important to keep an open mind with regards to what a *word*, *document* and *corpus* could actually refer to, depending on what the desired prediction entails.

As a basic approach, the count of each *word* in a *document* could be used to base the prediction, but this may not be the most accurate method. If each *document* can be guaranteed to have the same number of *words* in it, then this approach is adequate. But to account for *documents* that vary in size a more sensitive approach should be used.

This more sensitive approach comes from the idea of term frequency inverse document frequency *tf-idf*. There are two aspects to *tf-idf* - term frequency and inverse document frequency. Term frequency is more straightforward, and simply defines the proportion of times a word occurs in a document. Inverse document frequency is based on how many *documents* the word appears in while taking into account the number of *documents* in the *corpus*.

$$tf = \frac{number of times word appears in document}{number of words in document} \qquad (7.13)$$

$$idf = \log \frac{number of documents in corpus}{number of documents word appears in} \qquad (7.14)$$

tf-idf is the product of the two quantities, and is larger when the *word* appears frequently in a *document* with few *words*, or when the *word* appears in a very small number of *documents* in a large *corpus*. Recall from Chapter 3 that the data frame is the standard way in which to store our data ready to perform data science. If we calculate the *tf-idf* for every *word* in every *document* in a *corpus*, then the data frame will contain N rows for a *corpus* of N *documents*, and M columns for a *corpus* that contains M distinct *words*.

We will see how to apply *tf-idf* to classify samples of TCR sequences in Chapter 8.

7.6 Feature Selection

So far we have looked at building a predictive model using a set of manually chosen features. Whilst we might have used variables such as HBV viral load and necroinflammatory score to predict the presence or absence of HBeAg based on intuition, a data-driven approach combined with domain knowledge offers a better way to build an accurate model.

At first glance, you might think that the more features we include, the better the model is likely to be, as there is more information on which to make a correct prediction. In reality, introducing more features can complicate a model and increase the risk of overfitting. Overfitting occurs when a model is excessively complex, to the extent that it performs poorly on further observations. This poor performance occurs as it fails to generalise - it has been built to fit the training data set very closely, and does so very well because so many features were available to fit each nuance within the training set. But because these nuances are perhaps not present in new observations, the model performs poorly on them.

Of course, if every feature had the capability to predict the target accurately, overfitting would never occur. In reality, it occurs because some features are more useful than others in predicting the target. Thus an important aspect of building a predictive model is identifying which features have high predictive power. The added benefit of this selection is that our model becomes easier to interpret, as it uses fewer features on which to base the prediction.

What makes a good feature? To answer this, it's worth thinking about what makes a bad feature. A feature that has zero variance is an example of a poor predictor as a variable that never changes its value cannot be used to predict a target that does change its value.

The most straightforward approach in identifying which features to exclude comes from the idea of univariate feature selection. The principle is that we perform a test on each feature in turn, and score it according to some criteria. We can then keep the features with the highest scores, and exclude the rest.

The ANOVA test described in Chapter 4 can be used to assess the statistical significance between each feature and the target using the F-statistic. Fortunately, this is all neatly wrapped up in one function in Python's sklearn package, and is relatively easy to do in R as well. However, note that while Python returns the F-statistics itself (and so larger values are better), R returns the corresponding p-value (so smaller values imply a feature that is more predictive of the target variable).

```
def f_classif_score_function(X, y):
    return f_classif(X, y)

fs = SelectKBest(score_func=f_classif_score_function, k=3)
fs.fit(myData[features], myData[target])
fs.scores_
```

```
for (feature in features){
    print(paste(feature, anovaScores(myData[,feature], myData[,target]), sep=" "))
}
```

Out of the six features we used previously to predict the presence or absence of HBeAg (gMDSC, age, ALT, HBV viral load, HBsAg and necroinflammatory score), feature selection has enabled us to recognise the top three (sAg, viral load and age) of those six features which we should keep in our model, to make it more likely to generalise to new cases, as well as making it easier to interpret. We could of course have decided to keep only the top feature, and discard the rest - the decision of how many features to keep is a more complex process and an example of how to do this is given in Chapter 8.

A drawback of using the F-statistic from ANOVA to select features is that it only looks for linear relationships between the feature and target. A better approach is to use the mutual information between feature and target, as it captures more than just a linear dependence. In fact, it can capture any kind of relationship, and is therefore preferable to an ANOVA in most situations.

Mutual information addresses the question 'if I know the value of my feature, how much information does that give me in determining the value of the target?'. The mutual information between a discrete feature and discrete target is

$$I(X;Y) = \sum_y \sum_x p(x,y) log(\frac{p(x,y)}{p(x)p(y)}) \quad (7.15)$$

Larger values for mutual information imply the feature's value gives us more information on the what value the target might be. For example, if we were to calculate the mutual information between necroinflammatory score (a discrete feature) and presence/absence of HBeAg (a discrete target), we would first need to calculate the sum of probabilities of all possible combinations of necroinflammatory score (NI) and HBeAg (eAg); P(NI=1,eAg=+), P(NI=2,eAg=+),...,P(NI=7,eAg=-).

To calculate mutual information between a continuous variable and a discrete target, things get slightly more tricky, but can still be done. Figure 7.7 illustrates how this can be done, based on the original schematic in [36].

Now we have a basic understanding of how mutual information works, we can use it to select the top three features to predict the presence or absence of HBeAg.

```
def mutual_info_score_function(X, y):
    return mutual_info_classif(X, y, random_state=123)

fs = SelectKBest(score_func=mutual_info_score_function, k=3)
fs.fit(myData[features], myData[target])
fs.scores_
```

```
for (feature in features){
  print(paste(feature, mmi.pw(myData[,feature],myData[,target])$mi))
}
```

In this case, the selected features are the same as using the F-statistic (although HBV viral load is deemed to be the most important variable using mutual information). While univariate feature selection techniques are able to identify relationships between individual features and the target, they cannot capture the more

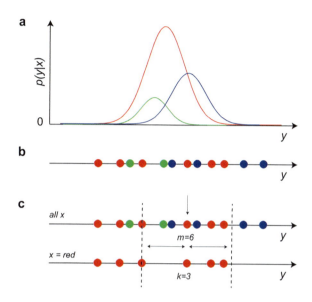

Figure 7.7: Mutual information can be used to determine how much information a continuous variable holds about another, categorical variable [36]. **a)** Hypothetical distribution of a continuous feature, which can take one of three categorical values, indicated in red, blue and green. **b** The distribution can be represented by placing each observation on a line, where the position on the line represents the value of the feature. **c)** A user-defined value of k is chosen ($k=3$ here). For each point, the distance of the third nearest neighbour of the same class (i.e. the distance of the third nearest point of the same class) is calculated (bottom line). The total number of points of all classes that lie within this distance is calculated (top line). A value I_i is calculated for the point in consideration based on what is called the digamma function. Mutual information is the average of I_i over the whole dataset. Larger values of mutual information will be found when more points of the same colour are co-localised on the line. This figure, along with this description of the method, has been reproduced from Ross (2014) [36].

complex interaction between multiple features that may increase predictive performance when used together. Thus, using such techniques may result in useful sets of features being excluded from our final model. An alternative approach exists in the form of recursive feature elimination (RFE). The concept is straightforward - begin by building a predictive model using all of the available features. Once the model is built, we iteratively eliminate the worst performing feature at each iteration. To be able to do this, we need to use a model that applies the concepts of 'weights' to classify variables. The weights associated with each feature are then compared and the worst is eliminated at each iteration. Typical models used to do this are SVM and logistic regression.

The process is stopped when the desired number of features is reached. An example of how to do this is given below, where we are looking to select the three top features.

```
selector = RFE(LinearSVC(random_state=123), n_features_to_select=3, step=1)
selector.fit( myData[features], myData[target])
features_selected = [ x for x,y in zip(features, selector.ranking_) if y==True]
features_selected
```

```
myData$eAglabel[myData$eAg==0] <- 'neg'
myData$eAglabel[myData$eAg==1] <- 'pos'
myChosenFeatures <- rfe(myData[,features],
    as.factor(myData[,"eAglabel"]),
    rfeControl=rfeControl(functions=caretFuncs, method='loocv'),
    method="svmLinear",
    size=3)
predictors(myChosenFeatures)
print(myChosenFeatures)
```

The chosen features using Python are viral load, sAg and NI score, while using R we find that age is also selected. It should be noted that while RFE in Python requires the user to define how many features they want to select, the process in R goes one step further and returns the number of features it deems optimal. The output from `myChosenFeatures` shows how the accuracy increases from 80% to 83% by including six features rather than just the three we originally told R that we were looking for (using `size=3`).

Chapter 8

Recipes

Throughout this book we have discussed the basic skills to put together small pieces of analysis. In this last Chapter, we have included some worked examples to put what we have learnt into practice.

8.1 Gene Expression

A full diagnosis of tumour origin when a patient presents in clinic can be a critical first step in driving treatment decisions. Gene expression profiling by DNA microarrays gives us a vast amount of data that would be hard to process manually. However, with the correct analytic technique, it also gives us the opportunity, for example, to distinguish between various acute cancer types. Thus, data science approaches can play a crucial role in a successful diagnosis.

This worked example is based on data collected by Golub et al. [4], and has been made freely available to the public. In the study, gene expression profiles were obtained from patients with acute myeloid leukemia (AML) and acute lymphoblastic leukemia (ALL), and a predictive model was built based on the individual gene expression profile of each patient. As with many gene expression datasets, we have many features (genes) on which to base a predictive model, and but relatively few patients. To begin such an analysis, the two important questions that need to be addressed in such a classification task are i) which features (genes) to use to build the predictive model and ii) how accurate is the model? For clinical diagnosis, the goal is likely to be establishing the minimum number of genes to provide a satisfactory model to accurately diagnose disease in patients (AML or ALL).

We have covered these topics in previous Chapters, so let's see how these ideas work in a real example. We will use Python in this case to attempt to answer these two questions, and we will use a linear support vector machine (SVM) to build the predictive model as it is well-suited to such data.

The first bit of code to write will load the various packages that we plan to use, and then read in our raw dataset which is stored in a *.csv* format. We can use the usual `read_csv` function from pandas to load the data ready to use.

```
import pandas as pd
import numpy as np

import matplotlib.pyplot as plt
import seaborn as sns
sns.set(style='white', font_scale=1.4)

from sklearn.feature_selection import RFE
from sklearn.svm import LinearSVC
from sklearn.model_selection import GridSearchCV, cross_val_predict, KFold, train_test_split
from sklearn.metrics import roc_auc_score, make_scorer, roc_curve, auc
from sklearn.preprocessing import label_binarize

data = pd.read_csv('/Users/yourname/Desktop/datascience/example1.csv')
```

Once we have loaded the dataset and necessary packages, we will need to define a few objects that will hold the results from our classification model. Lines 1 to 4 of the code below create such objects, using dictionaries to store our results in. This is often referred to as *initialising* variables ready for the main part of the example. `tpr` and `fpr` are dictionaries that will hold the true positive rate and false positive rate for various thresholds, for each distinct value in `gene_numbers`. The list called `gene_numbers` is something that we will iterate through, so that we can build a model with each of these numbers of genes, to see if we observe an improvement in the quality of our model as more genes are included. The final line of code is required as we will be choosing our model based on AUC rather than the default accuracy metric.

```
1  fpr = {}
2  tpr = {}
3  thresholds = {}
4  auc_scores = {}
5  gene_numbers = [1,10,20,50]
6  roc_scorer = make_scorer(roc_auc_score, greater_is_better=True, needs_threshold=True)
```

The main body of our code is based on a *for* loop, a grid search and K-fold cross validation. The *for* loop is used to investigate how our model performs when using a different number of genes. We use recursive feature elimination to identify the best n genes on which to build our model, so that we can determine how our model performs using these selected genes. Once we have identified which genes we are going to use at each iteration, GridSearchCV allows us to determine how our chosen model (linear SVM) performs for different values of C. Hyperparameter selection is a very important aspect of model selection. In Chapter 7 we chose $C = 1$ when we built our SVM (we did not need to define this as it is the default value given to C). We had no real reason to choose this value of C over any other value, and the best choice of C will vary from model to model, depending on the data that is being used. The framework that allows us to select the best value for C for our particular model is called a grid search.

It is absolutely imperative that you follow one rule when performing feature selection and/or hyperparameter selection - never test your model on any observation that you have used for feature selection or hyperparameter selection. If you break this rule, you risk developing an overly optimistic model that may not generalise well to new patients.

With these concepts in mind, the code below performs feature selection on one portion (split) of the data (containing 30% of all observations), (line 8), and splits the remaining data (70% of observations) into training and test sets. The training set is split into two folds, and the best value of C is determined on one fold of the data and performance is evaluated on the other fold of the data (lines 22 and 23). These two folds are then reversed, so that the best value of C is chosen from the two folds before being used on the test set.

```
for number_of_features in gene_numbers:

    ## FEATURE SELECTION
    ####################
    X = data.drop([ 'patient', 'cancer'], axis=1)
    y = data['cancer']

    X_fs, X_cv, y_fs, y_cv = train_test_split(X, y, test_size=0.7, random_state=123)

    selector = RFE(LinearSVC(random_state=123), n_features_to_select=number_of_features, step=500)
    selector.fit( X_fs, y_fs)

    genes = data.drop([ 'patient', 'cancer'], axis=1).columns
    chosen_genes = [gene for gene, support in zip(genes, selector.support_) if support==True]

    ## CROSS VALIDATION - CHOOSE OPTIMAL C & TEST
    ############################################
    X = X_cv[chosen_genes]
    y = label_binarize(y_cv, classes=['AML', 'ALL']).ravel()

    svm = LinearSVC(random_state=123)
    cv = KFold(n_splits=2, shuffle=True, random_state=123)
    model = GridSearchCV(estimator=svm, param_grid={"C": [1, 10, 100]}, cv=cv, scoring=roc_scorer)
    unformatted_scores = cross_val_predict(model, X=X, y=y, cv=cv, method='decision_function')
    scores = [item[1] for item in unformatted_scores ]

    fpr[number_of_features], tpr[number_of_features], thresholds[number_of_features] = roc_curve( y, scores )
    auc_scores[number_of_features] = auc(fpr[number_of_features], tpr[number_of_features])
```

Finally, now that we have the performance values (AUC) for our model using various numbers of genes, we can plot the ROC curve for each model. Plotting a ROC curve is not easily done in seaborn, so we will have to use the default plotting capability in matplotlib instead. This is done using the ax.plot() command once we have made a figure object using fig, ax = plt.subplots(). We use a loop to plot the results as we want to add a ROC curve at each iteration, using a different colour to plot each curve.

```
fig, ax = plt.subplots()
colours = ['red','navy','green', 'orange']

for number_of_features, colour in zip(gene_numbers, colours):
    ax.plot(fpr[number_of_features],
            tpr[number_of_features],
            color=colour,
            linestyle='-',
            label=str(number_of_features)+' Genes : AUC = {0:0.2f}'.format(auc_scores[number_of_features]))

ax.plot([0, 1], [0, 1], color='black', lw=2, linestyle=':')
ax.set_xlim([-0.05, 1.05])
ax.set_ylim([-0.05, 1.05])
ax.set_xlabel('FPR')
ax.set_ylabel('TPR')
plt.legend(bbox_to_anchor=(1, 0.5), loc='upper left', ncol=1)
sns.despine()
plt.show()
```

The results, shown in Figure 8.1 are intuitively what we might expect - a model using only one gene to make a prediction performs very poorly (AUC = 0.25), even if it is deemed the best single feature to predict tumour type. However, as we add more genes into the model, we can see that performance improves, as each curve moves more towards the top left hand corner of Figure 8.1. The dashed line represents a model that does no better than guessing, highlighting how badly the single gene model performs. However, the information provided by the expression of 20 genes is enough to get a respectable AUC of greater than 0.9. Finally, to answer the question above on which genes should be used to build the predictive model, see if you can amend the code above to print out the selected genes in each loop.

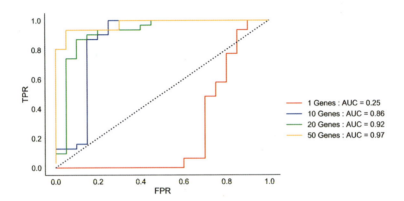

Figure 8.1: The inclusion of more genes improves the performance the predictive model to distinguish leukemia type. Recursive feature elimination (RFE) was used on all genes to determine the most predictive set of genes to include in the model. A grid search was used to determine the optimal value of the hyperparameter C for the linear SVM. Four ROC curves, which represent model accuracy, are shown for four models with differing number of genes used to make the prediction. In red, using only one predictive gene, the ROC curve gives an AUC of 0.25 and as such is unlikely to correctly stratify myeloid from lymphoblastic leukemia. Only the twenty most predictive genes are required to build an accurate model with AUC above 0.9.

8.2 Flow Cytometry

Flow cytometry is a commonly used technique in immunology to probe the characteristics of individual lymphocytes. Typically, once the data from a sample has been acquired, clustering can be used to determine the frequency and/or phenotype of each cell type in a sample.

This process normally requires the immunologist to define a sequential gating strategy to determine 'gates' to visualise cells of interest. However, this manual, sequential approach to gating is fundamentally biased and not always reproducible due to the subjective nature of gating individual samples. One way to reproduce the sequential gating approach used in programs such as FlowJo is to use an automated strategy to remove the subjective element of gating. This also has the advantage of being quicker when larger numbers of samples are being analysed with the same set of parameters.

Rather than developing your own automated gating strategy, the beauty of R and Python is that numerous packages exist that allow the community to make use of code developed by other programmers. For this particular example, we will use R and the excellent openCyto package developed by Finak et al. [37] that allows us to perform automated, data-driven gating in a sequential manner that will feel very familiar to the FlowJo user.

Traditional gating adopts a sequential, bivariate approach to detect known populations of interest. Hopefully after reading Chapter 5 it is apparent that this process of gating amounts to a clustering task. The user is essentially finding groups of events in 2D based on similarities in marker expression. Of the four approaches we covered in Chapter 5, openCyto adopts a distribution-based approach to finding such populations, assuming populations to be mixtures of t-distributions rather than the Gaussian distributions that were introduced in Chapter 5. Without going into too much detail on this matter, a t-distribution is similar in appearance to a Gaussian, with a key difference being that extreme values are more likely when a t-distribution is assumed. Combined with a Box-Cox transformation (a method that transforms data to make it resemble a normal distribution), this approach is better suited to typical flow cytometry data than a standard Gaussian distribution [38].

OpenCyto allows data-driven gating by defining clusters of interest, for example B cells, T cells and NK cells, before seeing the data. Populations can then be visualised using both the traditional approach of inspecting sequential 2D plots of phenotypic markers on our defined populations, such as the expression of activation markers. We can also project the populations into 2D space using tSNE.

For this example, we wil be using R, and we willl need to download and install the openCyto package using the following code.

```r
source("https://bioconductor.org/biocLite.R")
biocLite("openCyto")
```

Now we can analyse our *.fcs* file (the standard file format from cytometric analysers) using the following code. The openCyto uses the notion of a *gating template* - a spreadsheet that an immunologist can use to contain their desired gating strategy to identify cell populations of interest. Both the *.fcs* file and corresponding gating template are availale to download from our website. As always, make sure you change the code on line 5 to reflect your individual machine.

```r
library(openCyto)
library(Rtsne)
library(ggplot2)

setwd("/Users/yourname/Desktop/datascience/")
fcsFile <- "example2.fcs"

## READ IN T CELL GATING TEMPLATE
###############################
gating.template <- gatingTemplate("gatingtemplate.csv")


## READ IN FCS FILES
#################
samplesFlowSet <- read.flowSet(fcsFile, alter.names=TRUE)
sampleNames(samplesFlowSet) <- strsplit(fcsFile,".fcs")[[1]]

## COMPENSATION
##############
apply.compensation <- function(frame){
```

```
21  colnames(keyword(frame)$`SPILL`) <- gsub("-",".",colnames(keyword(frame)$`SPILL`))
22  colnames(keyword(frame)$`SPILL`) <- gsub(" ",".",colnames(keyword(frame)$`SPILL`))
23  comp <- keyword(frame)$`SPILL`
24  new_frame <- compensate(frame,comp)
25  new_frame
26  }
27
28  samplesFlowSet.comp <- fsApply(samplesFlowSet,apply.compensation)
29
30  ## REMOVE VARIABLES FSC, SSC .. FROM LOGICLE TRANSFORM
31  ##################################################
32  vars <- colnames(samplesFlowSet.comp)
33  vars <- vars[-grep("FSC",vars)]
34  vars <- vars[-grep("SSC",vars)]
35
36  ## TRANSFORM DATA USING LOGICLE TRANSFORM
37  ##########################################
38  lgcl <- estimateLogicle(samplesFlowSet.comp[[1]], channels = vars)
39  samplesFlowSet.trans <- transform(samplesFlowSet.comp, lgcl)
40
41  ## PERFORM AUTOMATED GATING
42  ############################
43  samples.gating.set <- GatingSet(samplesFlowSet.trans)
44  gating(gating.template, samples.gating.set, mc.cores=1, parallel_type = "multicore
        ")
45
46  ## GET POPULATION STATS
47  #######################
48  summary.stats.samples <- getPopStats(samples.gating.set[[1]])
49  summary.stats.samples
50
51  ## PLOT RESULTS
52  ###############
53  plotGate(samples.gating.set[[1]], xbin=50,default.y="SSC.A")
```

In our example, we defined a gating strategy to visualise multiple subsets of lymphocytes (B cells, T cells and NK cells). The populations that are found using this automated data-driven approach are shown in Figure 8.2. Once we have identified these populations, we need to tidy up the ouput and transform it into a data frame so that we can apply the techniques we have learnt about in previous Chapters.

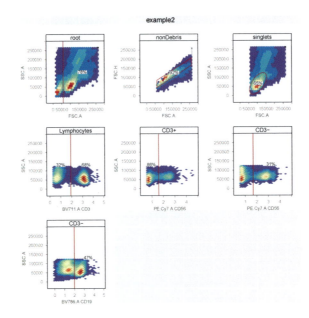

Figure 8.2: Example of a data-driven multiparametric flow cytometric analysis using the package OpenCyto and a predefined gating template to identify live, singlet lymphocytes from a human blood sample. The analysis allows the further identification of B cells (CD3-, CD19+), T cells (CD3+, CD56-) and NK cells (CD3-, CD56+) that can be used for further phenotypic analysis. Such an approach using automated data-driven gating can process hundreds of files in a matter of minutes on a standard specification machine.

To do this, we need to use two functions provided by openCyto - getData and exprs. This allows us to build up a data frame using only those events that have been gated as B cells, T cells or NK cells. Note that this approach is flexible enough to extract any population we want - simply alter the list called subsets to contain any of the populations listed in the *alias* column of the *gatingtemplate.csv*. Names in the *alias* column are the names we give to the defined populations when gating.

```
## GET DATA FRAME
#################
get.ab.names <- function(data){
  ab.names <- c()
  for (item in colnames(data)){
    if (is.na(getChannelMarker(data, item)$desc)){
      ab.names <- c(ab.names, getChannelMarker(data, item)$name)
    }
```

```
9        else {
10           ab.names <- c(ab.names, getChannelMarker(data, item)$desc)
11        }
12     }
13     return(ab.names)
14  }
15
16  subsets = c("Tcells", "NKcells", "Bcells")
17  df = data.frame()
18
19  for (pop in subsets){
20     myData = getData( samples.gating.set[[1]], pop)
21     values = exprs(myData)
22     df = rbind( df, values)
23  }
24
25  labels = c()
26  for (pop in subsets){
27     labels = c(labels, rep(pop, as.integer(dim(getData( samples.gating.set[[1]], pop
           ))[1])))
28  }
29
30  colnames(df) = get.ab.names(getData(samples.gating.set[[1]]))
31  df$Subset = labels
```

We have taken a *.fcs* file and have 'converted' this file into a data frame, the fundamental object of data science. We have relied on many of the functions provided by the `openCyto` package, and I would recommend reading the documentation for the package to fully understand these functions. We have also defined our own function called `get.ab.names`. This is a convenience function that is used to rename the columns of the data frame that we create - instead of using the fluorochrome labels that are used by default when we extract the event data, we replace fluorochrome labels with the correpsonding marker name in each case.

From here, we can now carry out further analysis using the techniques that have been introduced in the previous Chapters. In this case, we are going to reproduce the kind of visualisation that can be made using Cytobank's commercial tool, `viSNE`. So, we will use tSNE here, introduced in Chapter 6. As an example, let's visualise B cells, T cells and NK cells on the same plot (Figure 8.3).

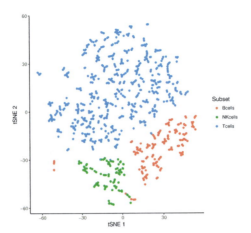

Figure 8.3: tSNE analysis to visualise the previously pre-gated multiparametric flow cytometric data of identified B cells, T cells and NK cells in a 2D plot. Unsurprisingly based on the markers used for tSNE, each cell type clusters separately due to their distinct expression profiles.

```
## tSNE
#######
sampled_df = df[sample(nrow(df), size=1000, replace=FALSE), ]

X = scale( sampled_df[, -which(names(df) == "Subset")], center = TRUE, scale = TRUE)
tsne = Rtsne(as.matrix(X), perplexity=3, pca=T, eta=100)
tsne_transformation = as.data.frame(tsne$Y)
tsne_transformation$Subset = sampled_df$Subset

g = ggplot(tsne_transformation, aes(x=V1, y=V2)) +
geom_point(aes(colour=Subset)) +
xlab("tSNE 1") +
ylab("tSNE 2") +
theme_bw()
g
```

Using tSNE, we have easily been able to stratify the three populations of cells that we were interested in. tSNE in itself is not an analytic technique, but can be useful in guiding the direction of further analysis. In Figure 8.3, we can see a small population of B cells that have been placed in a different location in the 2D visualisation compared to the majority of other B cells. Whilst this may not mean anything by itself, it warrants further analysis to determine if, and why, these cells have been located in a different region of the visualisation. This analysis is left as an exercise for the reader.

8.3 Sequencing

Next generation sequencing has given us unprecedented access to the immune system, giving us a greater understanding of B and T cell receptor repertoires than ever before. Whilst determining the specificity of individual T cell receptors (TCR) can be done through dextramer staining, this is difficult to scale to such an extent where we could determine the specificity of each TCR in each person. Thus, novel methods are required to reveal greater insights into the TCR repertoire.

A computational model that can accurately predict TCR specificity would be a great asset to the field of immunology, yet is an incredibly difficult challenge. Rather than building a generic predictive model that can predict the specificity of any given TCR, for this example let's focus on the more simple task of predicting whether a TCR is specific for HIV-1 or CMV. For this example, data comes from the brilliant TCR database (https://vdjdb.cdr3.net [39], which details epitope specificity for many TCR. The data used for this example has been downloaded directly from the database and can also be downloaded from our website.

For our final example, we will move back to Python and will use `TfidfVectorizer` in `sklearn` on which to base our analysis.

```
import pandas as pd
import numpy as np

from sklearn.feature_extraction.text import TfidfVectorizer
from sklearn.metrics import f1_score, make_scorer
from sklearn.preprocessing import label_binarize
from sklearn.decomposition import PCA
from sklearn.manifold import Isomap, TSNE
from sklearn.svm import LinearSVC
from sklearn.model_selection import GridSearchCV, cross_val_predict, KFold, train_test_split

import seaborn as sns
```

```
13  sns.set(style='white')
14  import matplotlib.pyplot as plt
15  %matplotlib inline
16
17  raw_data = pd.read_csv('/Users/yourname/Desktop/datascience/example3.txt',sep="\t"
        )
18  epitope1 = 'CMV'
19  epitope2 = 'HIV-1'
20  f1_scorer = make_scorer(f1_score)
```

Once we have imported the necessary packages, we read the data in and define our own scoring function like we did in the first example. In this case, we will be using the F1 score to determine how accurate our model is. Note that we are reading a *.txt* file on this occasion, so we need to modify our `read_csv` accordingly using the argument `sep="\t"`.

```
1  cdr3 = raw_data[raw_data['Epitope species'].isin([epitope1,epitope2])][['CDR3','
       Epitope species']]
2  cdr3 = cdr3.sample(frac=1)
3  cdr3.head()
```

After loading the raw data, we create a new data frame that only contains CDR3 data for TCR that are specific for the two epitopes we are interested in (CMV or HIV-1). The second line here is necessary to ensure that the data are randomised for cross validation later on - the raw data seems to be ordered by epitope specificity in this example here, which necessitates this line of code. We now set up our classification problem by converting the CDR3 amino acid sequences into 'documents' where each 'word' in the document is an amino acid. The corpus is then the collection of all CDR3 sequences. We want to learn a model which predicts which 'documents' are HIV-1-specific and which CMV-specific.

```
1  X = cdr3[['CDR3']]
2  y = label_binarize(cdr3['Epitope species'], classes=[epitope1,epitope2]).ravel()
3
4  X_train, X_test, y_train, y_test = train_test_split(X, y, test_size=0.5, random_
       state=123)
5
6  corpus_train = [seq for seq in X_train['CDR3'].tolist()]
```

```
7  model = TfidfVectorizer(analyzer='char', lowercase=False, ngram_range=(1,1))
8  matrix_train = model.fit_transform(corpus_train).todense()
```

We use `train_test_split` to create our training and test sets, and generate our training corpus from every CDR3 sequence in the training set. For use with `TfidfVectorizer`, the corpus must be a list of strings, where each string is a separate document (i.e. corpus is a list of strings where each string is a CDR3 sequence). The last two lines of code transform the corpus into a matrix where the rows represent observations (each TCR CDR3 sequence) and the columns represent the features (the TfIdf of each amino acid in each CDR3 sequence). It is important to note the use of `ngram_range` here - n-grams are all subsequences of n amino acids of length n. For example, 2-grams of the sequence *CASS* would be *CA, AS, SS*. The use of n-grams generates more features on which to base a prediction, potentially giving the model more predictive power. Once you have run this example, try amending the code below to build a model that uses 2-grams as well as single amino acids by changing `ngram_range=(1,2)`.

Once we have converted our sequence data into a numerical representation of sequences, we can use the usual approach to training and testing our model through grid search and cross validation.

```
1  svm = LinearSVC(random_state=123)
2  cv = KFold(n_splits=2, shuffle=True)
3  model = GridSearchCV(estimator=svm, param_grid={"C": [1, 10, 100]}, cv=cv, scoring
       =f1_scorer)
4  model.fit(matrix_train, y_train)
5  best_model = model.best_estimator_
6  best_model
```

Using grid search, we can identify the best model and use it to test on the remaining test set. In this example, due to the fact that we had a large number of observations (use `.shape` on the data frame to determine exactly how many observations), we are able to split training and testing into two distinct folds.

```
1  corpus_test = [seq for seq in X_test['CDR3'].tolist()]
2  model = TfidfVectorizer(analyzer='char', lowercase=False, ngram_range=(1,1))
3  matrix_test = model.fit_transform(corpus_test).todense()
```

```
predictions = cross_val_predict( best_model, matrix_test, y_test, cv=3)
f1_score( y_test, predictions)
```

Finally, testing our model to make predictions of epitope specificity of each TCR CDR3, we get an F1 score of 0.81, which tells us that we have built a fairly accurate model that can distinguish between HIV-1-specific TCR and CMV-specific TCR.

Afterword

Thanks for buying and reading the book, we hope you have found it useful.

For any comments or questions, please get in touch with us through email or Twitter and we will be more than happy to help or listen to feedback. Contact details are available on our website.

Bibliography

[1] information explosion | Definition of information explosion in English by Oxford Dictionaries.

[2] Clive Humby. Why Do People Still Think Data Is the New Oil?, January 2018.

[3] A singularity sensation - Author Vernor Vinge talks sci-fi health care - 2012 SUMMER - Stanford Medicine Magazine - Stanford University School of Medicine.

[4] T. R. Golub, D. K. Slonim, P. Tamayo, C. Huard, M. Gaasenbeek, J. P. Mesirov, H. Coller, M. L. Loh, J. R. Downing, M. A. Caligiuri, C. D. Bloomfield, and E. S. Lander. Molecular classification of cancer: class discovery and class prediction by gene expression monitoring. *Science (New York, N.Y.)*, 286(5439):531–537, October 1999.

[5] Jennifer K Roe, Niclas Thomas, Eliza Gil, Katharine Best, Evdokia Tsaliki, Stephen Morris-Jones, Sian Stafford, Nandi Simpson, Karolina D Witt, Benjamin Chain, Robert F Miller, Adrian Martineau, and Mahdad Noursadeghi. Blood transcriptomic diagnosis of pulmonary and extrapulmonary tuberculosis. *JCI Insight*, 1(16).

[6] James M. Heather, Katharine Best, Theres Oakes, Eleanor R. Gray, Jennifer K. Roe, Niclas Thomas, Nir Friedman, Mahdad Noursadeghi, and Benjamin Chain. Dynamic Perturbations of the T-Cell Receptor Repertoire in Chronic HIV Infection and following Antiretroviral Therapy. *Frontiers in Immunology*, 6, January 2016.

[7] Niclas Thomas, Katharine Best, Mattia Cinelli, Shlomit Reich-Zeliger, Hilah Gal, Eric Shifrut, Asaf Madi, Nir Friedman, John Shawe-Taylor, and Benny

Chain. Tracking global changes induced in the CD4 T-cell receptor repertoire by immunization with a complex antigen using short stretches of CDR3 protein sequence. *Bioinformatics (Oxford, England)*, 30(22):3181–3188, November 2014.

[8] Derrick Baxby. Edward Jenner's Inquiry; a bicentenary analysis. *Vaccine*, 17(4):301–307, February 1999.

[9] Emil von Behring. Emil von Behring - Nobel Lecture: Serum Therapy in Therapeutics and Medical Science.

[10] James M. Heather and Benjamin Chain. The sequence of sequencers: The history of sequencing DNA. *Genomics*, 107(1):1–8, January 2016.

[11] Edward S. Lee, Paul G. Thomas, Jeff E. Mold, and Andrew J. Yates. Identifying T Cell Receptors from High-Throughput Sequencing: Dealing with Promiscuity in TCRalpha and TCRbeta Pairing. *PLOS Computational Biology*, 13(1):e1005313, January 2017.

[12] Katharine Best, Theres Oakes, James M. Heather, John Shawe-Taylor, and Benny Chain. Computational analysis of stochastic heterogeneity in PCR amplification efficiency revealed by single molecule barcoding. *Scientific Reports*, 5:14629, October 2015.

[13] Olga V. Britanova, Ekaterina V. Putintseva, Mikhail Shugay, Ekaterina M. Merzlyak, Maria A. Turchaninova, Dmitriy B. Staroverov, Dmitriy A. Bolotin, Sergey Lukyanov, Ekaterina A. Bogdanova, Ilgar Z. Mamedov, Yuriy B. Lebedev, and Dmitriy M. Chudakov. Age-Related Decrease in TCR Repertoire Diversity Measured with Deep and Normalized Sequence Profiling. *The Journal of Immunology*, 192(6):2689–2698, March 2014.

[14] Evaggelia Liaskou, Eva Kristine Klemsdal Henriksen, Kristian Holm, Fatemeh Kaveh, David Hamm, Janine Fear, Marte K. Viken, Johannes Roksund Hov, Espen Melum, Harlan Robins, Johanna Olweus, Tom H. Karlsen, and Gideon M. Hirschfield. High-throughput T-cell receptor sequencing across chronic liver diseases reveals distinct disease-associated repertoires. *Hepatology*, 63(5):1608–1619, May 2016.

[15] James M. Heather, Mazlina Ismail, Theres Oakes, and Benny Chain. High-throughput sequencing of the T-cell receptor repertoire: pitfalls and opportunities. *Briefings in Bioinformatics*.

[16] Joseph Kaplinsky and Ramy Arnaout. Robust estimates of overall immune-repertoire diversity from high-throughput measurements on samples. *Nature Communications*, 7:11881, June 2016.

[17] J. Paul Robinson. Wallace H. Coulter: Decades of invention and discovery. *Cytometry Part A*, 83A(5):424–438, May 2013.

[18] Regina K. Cheung and Paul J. Utz. Screening: CyTOF - the next generation of cell detection. *Nature Reviews Rheumatology*, 7(9):502, September 2011.

[19] A. L. Samuel. Some Studies in Machine Learning Using the Game of Checkers. *IBM Journal of Research and Development*, 3(3):210–229, July 1959.

[20] John P. A. Ioannidis. Why Most Published Research Findings Are False. *PLOS Medicine*, 2(8):e124, August 2005.

[21] David McCandless: The Beauty of Data Visualization - Blog, September 2013.

[22] Thomas H. Davenport and D. J. Patil. Data Scientist: The Sexiest Job of the 21st Century, October 2012.

[23] Enda Ridge. Guerrilla Analytics, September 2014.

[24] Hadley Wickham. Tidy Data.

[25] Laura J. Pallett, Upkar S. Gill, Alberto Quaglia, Linda V. Sinclair, Maria Jover-Cobos, Anna Schurich, Kasha P. Singh, Niclas Thomas, Abhishek Das, Antony Chen, Giuseppe Fusai, Antonio Bertoletti, Doreen A. Cantrell, Patrick T. Kennedy, Nathan A. Davies, Muzlifah Haniffa, and Mala K. Maini. Metabolic regulation of hepatitis B immunopathology by myeloid-derived suppressor cells. *Nature Medicine*, 21(6):591–600, June 2015.

[26] Jeffrey Stanton. Galton, Pearson, and the Peas: A Brief History of Linear Regression for Statistics Instructors. *Journal of Statistics Education*, 9, January 2001.

[27] J. MacQueen. Some methods for classification and analysis of multivariate observations. The Regents of the University of California, 1967.

[28] Martin Ester, Hans-Peter Kriegel, Jorg Sander, and Xiaowei Xu. A density-based algorithm for discovering clusters in large spatial databases with noise. pages 226–231. AAAI Press, 1996.

[29] J. B. Tenenbaum, V. de Silva, and J. C. Langford. A global geometric framework for nonlinear dimensionality reduction. *Science (New York, N.Y.)*, 290(5500):2319–2323, December 2000.

[30] Laurens van der Maaten and Geoffrey Hinton. Visualizing Data using t-SNE. *Journal of Machine Learning Research*, 9(Nov):2579–2605, 2008.

[31] El-ad David Amir, Kara L. Davis, Michelle D. Tadmor, Erin F. Simonds, Jacob H. Levine, Sean C. Bendall, Daniel K. Shenfeld, Smita Krishnaswamy, Garry P. Nolan, and Dana Pe'er. viSNE enables visualization of high dimensional single-cell data and reveals phenotypic heterogeneity of leukemia. *Nature Biotechnology*, 31(6):545, June 2013.

[32] R. A. Fisher. The Use of Multiple Measurements in Taxonomic Problems. *Annals of Eugenics*, 7(2):179–188, September 1936.

[33] Leo Breiman. Random Forests. *Machine Learning*, 45(1):5–32, October 2001.

[34] Nello Cristianini and John Shawe-Taylor. *An Introduction to Support Vector Machines: And Other Kernel-based Learning Methods*. Cambridge University Press, New York, NY, USA, 2000.

[35] David Cox. The regression analysis of binary sequences (with discussion). *J Roy Stat Soc B*, 20:215–242, 1958.

[36] Brian C. Ross. Mutual Information between Discrete and Continuous Data Sets. *PLOS ONE*, 9(2):e87357, February 2014.

[37] Greg Finak, Jacob Frelinger, Wenxin Jiang, Evan W. Newell, John Ramey, Mark M. Davis, Spyros A. Kalams, Stephen C. De Rosa, and Raphael Gottardo. OpenCyto: An Open Source Infrastructure for Scalable, Robust, Reproducible, and Automated, End-to-End Flow Cytometry Data Analysis. *PLOS Computational Biology*, 10(8):e1003806, August 2014.

[38] Kenneth Lo, Florian Hahne, Ryan R. Brinkman, and Raphael Gottardo. flowClust: a Bioconductor package for automated gating of flow cytometry data. *BMC bioinformatics*, 10:145, May 2009.

[39] Mikhail Shugay, Dmitriy V. Bagaev, Ivan V. Zvyagin, Renske M. Vroomans, Jeremy Chase Crawford, Garry Dolton, Ekaterina A. Komech, Anastasiya L. Sycheva, Anna E. Koneva, Evgeniy S. Egorov, Alexey V. Eliseev, Ewald Van Dyk, Pradyot Dash, Meriem Attaf, Cristina Rius, Kristin Ladell, James E. McLaren, Katherine K. Matthews, E. Bridie Clemens, Daniel C. Douek, Fabio Luciani, Debbie van Baarle, Katherine Kedzierska, Can Kesmir, Paul G. Thomas, David A. Price, Andrew K. Sewell, and Dmitriy M. Chudakov. VDJdb: a curated database of T-cell receptor sequences with known antigen specificity. *Nucleic Acids Research*, 46(D1):D419–D427, January 2018.

Printed in Poland
by Amazon Fulfillment
Poland Sp. z o.o., Wrocław